from Political Islam,
China, Russia,
Pandemics, and
Racial Strife

THE MULTIFRONT WAR

Kenneth Abramowitz

THE MULTIFRONT WAR

Defending America from Political Islam, China, Russia, Pandemics, and Racial Strife

Kenneth Abramowitz

Washington, DC

THE MULTIFRONT WAR. Copyright © 2020 by Kenneth Abramowitz. All rights reserved.

No part of this publication may be reproduced, stored in a retrieval system, or transmitted in any form or by any means, including electronic, mechanical, photocopying, recording, scanning, or otherwise, except as permitted under Section 107 or 108 of the 1976 United States Copyright Act. Permissions requests to the publisher should be addressed to permissions@dialogpress.com.

The paperback edition of this book is printed on acid-free paper.

Paperback ISBN: 978-0-914153-82-5
eBook ISBN: 978-0-914153-53-5
Printed in the United States of America.
15 14 13 12 11 5 4 3 2 1

Cover design and art direction by Myles Hoenes.
Page design and typesetting by E. M. Jones.

Modern book text is produced using a variety of collaborative software tools, including automated spellcheckers and text revision tools. It is possible for such software to create typographical errors or other textual changes beyond the control of the author, editors, or publisher. Please report errors to errata@dialogpress.com; changes, corrections, and additions can be found at https://multifrontwar.com.

URLs, titles, and statistics were accurate as of press time; neither the author nor the publisher is responsible for pages or other resources that have expired or moved since the manuscript was prepared.

To Nira, my loving wife, who stood by me throughout all the challenges of producing this work.

Table of Contents

Foreword: Reassessing Our Threats *Walid Phares*	v
Introduction and Acknowledgements	xi
Notes on Usage	xvii
Image Credits	xxi
Chapter One: Confronting the Multifront War	1
Chapter Two: False Narratives	11
Chapter Three: The Islamist Hydra	31
Chapter Four: Israel's Success Story	43
Chapter Five: America's Willful Blindness	57
Chapter Six: The Accelerating Islamization of Europe	69
Chapter Seven: Stopping Iran	81
Chapter Eight: China Ascending, Russia Resurging	89
Chapter Nine: The Rise of the Radical Left in the US	99
Chapter Ten: Defeating Political Islam	109
Chapter Eleven: Solving Problems, Implementing Solutions	115
Chapter Twelve: COVID-19's Consequences	129
Chapter Thirteen: Winning the Multifront War	135
Afterword: When the Smoke of 9/11 Cleared *Rachel Ehrenfeld*	141
Further Reading	149

Foreword: Reassessing Our Threats
Walid Phares

World affairs have evolved on many levels. In a post-Cold War, post-9/11, post-Arab Spring, and post-Iran Nuclear Deal world, international relations and international security must be reevaluated as concepts and lucidly re-explained to the public. Challenges have changed. Balances of power have shifted. Political philosophies have mutated. Most importantly, the capacities for the public and individual citizens to understand, transfer information, and take action have dramatically evolved during the first quarter of the twenty-first century.

In this wave of new analysts rolling onto the global stage, Kenneth Abramowitz emerges as an author with a special hybrid message, piercing through the classic and often obsolete assertions of academia and media regarding the threats moving against the free world in general and the transatlantic bloc and its allies in other areas of the world. As an economist and healthcare strategic expert, he brings in the social mathematics of people's needs. As a global stability analyst, he matches the latter needs to the actual geopolitical equations in their raw reality.

In *The Multifront War*, his new, well-conceived book, Abramowitz lays out the structural map of the conflicts that have been raging since the fall of the Berlin wall.

He accurately notes that a fog of war is obstructing a clear vision for the public as mainstream media and its ideological sources are suppressing facts and objective assessment of crises and developments. Indeed, as I warned in my 2007 book, *The War of Ideas*, an intellectual elite is now blocking access to real information. This elite distills what matches their interests—and the interests of the people who fund them. Hence, books like Abramowitz's, and others, are shattering the thick crust of the false narrative obstructing that knowledge.

The jihadist threat sits atop all other menaces; the goal of such an ideology is the sheer annihilation of all other visions and dominance worldwide. The Takfiri Salafist ideology in the Sunni world and the Khomeinist doctrine in the Shia sphere have been escalating for decades. But it was after the Cold War that they expanded in numbers of followers, seized territory, and expanded their influence in the Greater Middle East and beyond. The September 11, 2001 attacks on US soil prompted the United States to respond with counterterrorism measures overseas, starting in Afghanistan and Iraq and then reaching across the globe. This "long war" has had ground successes against the Taliban, al-Qaeda, and other groups for 19 years, but has been undermined by shortcomings at the policy and strategy levels. In recent years, however, US military power has been neither served nor deployed well by American political thinking, itself influenced by radicals.

Abramowitz's work is a reminder that the conceptual part of the War on Terror has failed. Because America has been attacked on multiple fronts, the war against these threats must also take place on multiple fronts. The US defensive posture against the global jihadist threat, described as "political Islam" by the author of the book, must be as complex as the threat itself. I have been calling for the rise of strategic counters to the jihadi menace for decades, not only against ISIS or al-Qaeda, but moving deeper into the ideological realm and pushing for de-radicalization and de-indoctrination. As I have argued to intelligence and counterterrorism analysts and officials for decades, only by defeating indoctrination efforts can we win the kinetic wars.

But lobbying efforts by militant networks such as the Muslim Brotherhood have caused tremendous delays in US mobilization efforts since 2001. Building a defense strategy against the Iranian regime component of the jihadi forces has been even more challenging. Though US power, especially under the Trump administration, has boxed in Iran's most recent expansion, the negative effects of the Iran Nuclear Deal, conceived under the Obama administration, have already empowered Tehran to continue strategic advances and to target US allies in the region. The impact of Iran's activities can be seen from Israel to the Arab Coalition, while also targeting Americans in the Middle East. The Iranian front is the most dangerous and imminent. But the US is also engaged in several other challenging tracks.

The peace process between Israel and the Arab world has been a challenge for multiple US administrations, hindering stability in the region, serving as propaganda material for radicals and terrorists, and diverting most advancement in the Arab world into wars and conflicts. Recent efforts by Washington to enlist new partners in peace—the UAE,

Bahrain, and soon more countries—under the umbrella of the Abraham Accords, demonstrate that the conflict on this front can be based on strong relations between Washington, Israel, and the Arab Coalition. For decades, and twice as a foreign policy advisor to presidential candidates, I saw today's reality as an emerging possibility, because both Arab moderates and Israelis have been ready to achieve this goal for years. For their part, Palestinians can be guaranteed their rights, but only after Iranian and Muslim Brotherhood influences within their communities begin to recede.

The next front reveals radical networks attempting to manipulate organized refugee thrusts into the West. Instead of finding solutions to social, political and economic crises in their homelands, Islamist and neo-Marxist groups have been trying to push mass refugee migrations from the Mediterranean towards Europe, and from South America towards the US borders. The extremists' control of the refugees' recruitment process breaks humanitarian principles and exacerbates conflicts in Europe and the Western Hemisphere. American immigration policies are now challenged and politicized by anti-American forces.

Economic wars are also becoming new fronts. Previous US administrations opened the international gates to extreme empowerment of Beijing within the international financial system without obtaining significant political advancements for its population. This also allowed increasing US economic dependency on China. Relations with Russia have also deteriorated, particularly since Moscow's now-challenged backing of the Iranian and Assad regimes in the Middle East.

Back to the US, the ascendency of a radical left with neo-Marxist platforms, caused by a radicalization of academia over the past few decades, has created an intellectual and cultural front, harming American liberal pluralism. Indeed, US leadership is facing a multi-front strategic challenge, and a new generation of intellectual responses is now needed to provide guidance to the public. The national security of the United States needs fresh thinking to adapt to the emerging challenges, and Abramowitz's book is a well-thought-out attempt to refocus America's responses.

Walid Phares
Washington, DC
October 2, 2020

Dr. Walid Phares was a foreign policy advisor to presidential candidates Donald Trump and Mitt Romney and is a national security analyst for Fox News. He is the author of The Choice, Future Jihad, War of Ideas, *and* The Lost Spring.

Introduction and Acknowledgements

The brazen attack by al-Qaeda on New York City's Twin Towers on September 11, 2001 killed nearly 3,000 Americans, injured 25,000, and sent shockwaves throughout America and all the world. Those shockwaves are still being felt today; although, as time goes by, fewer and fewer people remember. Nonetheless, that attack triggered the wheels of my mind.

As a professional analyst of the healthcare industry, I immediately redirected my six-day-per-week work schedule to dedicate one day each week to national security analysis. I did this simply as a concerned citizen. Then, witnessing the disastrous Iran Nuclear Deal in 2015, I stepped up my time commitment to two days per week. As, week after week, I witnessed the multitude of low-quality national security analysts on mass media and social media, I made the decision to codify my thoughts in a book-length work that would address the threats to Western Civilization and the fight ahead as a multifront war ramped up.

As I assemble my thanks to the many who gave me intellectual, professional, and personal support, I focus first on motivation. Here I aptly thank the fake news mainstream media for hiring "talking heads" with particularly poor analytical skills, who then invited biased "experts" in various specific disciplines who could not see the big picture of challenges that we continue to face. I also witnessed the major social media platforms increasingly censor the conservative voices who believe in the Constitution, while neglecting the escalating hateful rhetoric of the socialists, communists, anarchists, and Islamists. These accumulating echoes of misinformation further encouraged me to seek truth and accuracy in the face of this massive onslaught of fake, distorted news.

I thank about 150 authors who shared their historical knowledge with me—knowledge that helped me hone my ideas. These authors were experts in their fields, albeit in silos of knowledge. Their siloed expertise encouraged me to bridge gaps and unify threat assessments in this multifront war.

Likewise, I would thank the top 100 national security think tanks in the Western world and some 200 of their key researchers who worked so hard to educate me and the general public through their informative websites and webinars. I would also like to thank the nearly 100 senators, representatives, governors, and White House advisers, as well as their counterparts in Europe and Israel, who shared their perspectives with me.

Most authors, when finishing their first books, look back on their education and thank their parents. Now I understand why. I pause to remember my parents, William and Lee, and thank them for sending me for to the Taft School in Watertown, Connecticut, where I learned to read and write in a critical manner. My time at Columbia University provided me with a core curriculum of Western civilization's literature, philosophy, and history. My parents also encouraged me to attend Harvard Business School, where I further developed my analytical skills. My journey into critical thinking owes much to my parents' foresight.

My extensive academic training enabled me to apply professional analysis in a real-world career. It began with 23 years at a leading brokerage firm, followed by three years at the Carlyle Group, a private equity fund manager, and then 17 more years at healthcare venture capital fund manager NGN Capital.

Migrating my national security analysis to paper was pivotally assisted by renowned researchers Rachel Ehrenfeld and Nicholas Di'Iorio. Along the way, I developed a website, SaveTheWest.com, which reflects my thoughts. Here, my website managers, Jon Sutz and Ilana Freedman, are due all the credit, along with my social media manager, Arik Gerber, my media consultant Aryeh Werth, and particularly my skillful assistant for 35 years (since my early days at Sanford C. Bernstein & Co., Inc.), Noreen Harten.

All authors thank their publishers and editors, but every page of this book was indeed expertly managed by my publishers at Dialog Press and my sage editors, including Eve Jones in New York, Martin Barillas in Detroit, Nick Charles in London, Chris Hamel in Vancouver, BC, Christine Randolph in Indianapolis, and Carol Black in Washington, DC. Graphic artist Myles Hoenes uplifted the work with his brilliant cover and graphical concepts. Their collective work was more than production—they made the crucial difference between mere opinions and reasoning steeped in a historical and global context.

Above all, I must thank my wife, Nira, who challenged my thoughts and patiently supported my efforts through years of formation from impressed ideas to printed page.

Kenneth Abramowitz
Palm Beach
October 1, 2020

Notes on Usage

When discussing global topics, one often encounters numerous and confusing spellings of the same name, city, or religious precept. These names are so divergent that the uninitiated might think different individuals, locations or principles are being referenced.

For example, the name of the holy book of Islam is transliterated to English as Koran, Quran, Qur'an, and other variants; its author as Mohammed, Muhammad, and so on; the terror organization that pursued a new caliphate as IS, ISIS, ISIL, and DAESH; the Shia Islamist political "party of God" as Hezbollah, Hizbollah, Hezballah, Hisbollah, Hizbu'llah, and Hizb Allah.

To avoid confusion, we have standardized, to the best of our ability, all spellings in the text, except where a change would interfere with a title or context. In addition, original spellings have been retained in direct quotes. In the main, we adhered to the *Chicago Manual of Style* for style decisions, including the omission of periods from acronyms.

This book was finalized in the autumn of 2020. Trends, statistics, and facts set forth were accurate as of that time.

Selected Acronyms and Abbreviations

ACA	The Affordable Care Act (Obamacare)
CFPB	Consumer Financial Protection Board
COVID-19	The illness caused by the novel coronavirus SARS-CoV2
EPA	Environmental Protection Agency
ISIS	Islamic State of Iraq and Syria
JCPOA	Joint Comprehensive Plan of Action (the Iran Nuclear Deal)
MB	Muslim Brotherhood
NGO	Non-governmental organization
OIC	Organization of Islamic Cooperation
OPEC	Organization of the Petroleum Exporting Countries
PA	Palestinian Authority
PLO	Palestine Liberation Organization
UAE	United Arab Emirates
UNRWA	United Nations Relief and Works Agency
WHO	World Health Organization

Image Credits

A variety of striking images was used in this book. The editors in consultation with graphics designers Myles Hoenes and E.M. Jones created a graphical logic. Statues of individuals or personified concepts were selected to open chapters; objects were selected to open the front and back matter.

All images of statues were cropped to focus on their faces; all are located in the US except for the illustration for the COVID-19 chapter, which comes from Great Britain (as the pandemic is global). Often, but not always, there was a thematic relevance to the image selection.

All photos were taken from royalty-free, publicly available collections. Note that appearance of an image in this book does not in any way imply the photographer's endorsement of the content of this book.

Image Details and Credits

ToC: The Liberty Bell, Independence National Historical Park, Philadelphia – Cast by the Whitechapel Foundry; photo: Jared Kofsky

Foreword: US Capitol Building Dome – Cast by the Foundry of Janes, Fowler, Kirtland & Company; photo Sox524

Introduction: Tribute in Light, NYC, 2010 – John Bennett, Gustavo Bonevardi, Richard Nash Gould,

Julian LaVerdiere, Paul Myoda, and Paul Marantz (lighting consultant); photo: Sgt Randall A. Clinton

Notes on Usage: Metal Type – Imprimerie PAM, Brest; photo: G. Mannaerts

Image Credits: Stanley Kubrick's Speed Graphic camera at the LACMA exhibit; photo: Seth Anderson

Chapter One: Liberty Enlightening the World, Statue of Liberty National Monument, NYC – Auguste Bartholdi and Gustave Eiffel; photo Momentmal

Chapter Two: Abraham Lincoln, Lincoln Memorial, Washington, DC – Daniel French and the Piccirilli Brothers; photo: Rachel Bostwick

Chapter Three: George Washington, Mount Rushmore National Memorial, Keystone, SD – Gutzon Borglum; photo: Scott Catron

Chapter Four: Albert Einstein, Albert Einstein Memorial, National Academy of Sciences, DC – Robert Berks, cast by Modern Art Foundry; photo: Charles Raywriter

Chapter Five: Benjamin Franklin, Franklin Institute, Philadelphia – James Earle Fraser; photo: Peter Clerking

Chapter Six: Atlas, Rockefeller Center, NYC – Lee Lawrie with Rene Paul Chambellan; photo: Caroline Steinhauer

Chapter Seven: Freedom (or Columbia) on top of the US Capitol Dome, DC – Thomas Crawford; photo: Carol M. Highsmith, Carol M. Highsmith Archive, Library of Congress

Chapter Eight: John F. Kennedy, Grand Army Plaza, NYC – Neil Estern; photo: OpenCooper

Chapter Nine: Frederick Douglass, Douglass Circle, NYC – Gabriel Koren; photo: Jay Dobkin

Chapter Ten: Thomas Jefferson, Monticello – Stuart Williamson under the direction of Ivan Schwartz; photo: David Broad

Chapter Eleven: The Stone of Hope (Dr. Martin Luther King, Jr), Martin Luther King, Jr Memorial, DC – Lei Yixin; photo: olekinderhook

Chapter Twelve: Mary Seacole, St Thomas's Hospital, London – Martin Jennings; photo: Sumit Surai

Chapter Thirteen: Dwight D. Eisenhower – Zenos Frudakis (sculpture and photo)

Afterword: Unisphere at the 1964 World's Fairgrounds, NYC – Gilmore David Clarke; photo: dluger

Further Reading: Fortitude (one of the lions that guards the NYPL's main branch; the other is named Patience), NYC – Edward Clark Potter and The Piccirilli Brothers; photo: C.S. Imming

Chapter One: Confronting the Multifront War

America is fighting World War III. But our leaders do not seem to know it. Moreover, this war is being waged on a multitude of distinct fronts—internal and external. It is a multifront war that we must confront.

Internally, the country is under attack along an array of distinct fronts. First, we see play-to-win "big government" and "deep state" progressive leftists. Second, isolationists want to constrain our role in a world teeming with our adversaries. Third, foreign-oriented globalists want to dilute and weaken us from within. Fourth, 2020 saw a well-planned anarchic, revolutionary, Marxist, socialist hijacking of peaceful protests over the excruciating videoed police murder of George Floyd. Quickly, the marchers were subsumed by organized arson, insurrection, looting, and infiltration of local governance by calculated anarchic subversion.

Fifth, our biggest internal challenge, both culturally and physically, arises from political Islam, waged domestically but often a proxy for synergistic forces abroad. Political Islam—*Islamism*—represents the politicization of a religion, and we have eschewed any strategy to deal with this threat. Knowledgeable people realize that the religion of Islam is one of several Abrahamic monotheistic belief systems, and one that is protected by our Constitution. However, the politicization of Islam through the imposition of Sharia and jihad is not protected. It is, in fact, subversive to our laws, our country, and our very way of life.

History teaches that religion has from time to time melded and morphed into political extremism and military adventurism—from the Crusades that swept across Europe and the Middle East to Northern Ireland, where nationalists clashed in the years of unrest euphemistically called "The Troubles." The world has seen such manifestations often enough to differentiate between religious practice and religious militarism. Ironically, most Arab and Muslim-majority countries have long ago drawn a clear line between the Islamic religion and Islamic extremism. Many Arab and Muslim countries worldwide have outlawed Islamist groups.

Externally, we are challenged by Communist China's undisguised party primacy coupled with Vladimir Putin's authoritarian vision masquerading as a democracy in Russia. Simultaneously and unfortunately in 2020, the COVID-19 pandemic has consumed, and will continue to consume, huge governmental time and financial resources. As devastating as any armed conflict, the virus has unleashed another front, a permeating, omnipresent front, which must be combated everywhere at once by every scientific, economic, and good governance resource available.

Yes, America is racing to combat individual threats with various independent strategies. Yet, it is still not facing up to them as combined challenges and developing the integrated strategy to repel and prevail in the multifront war now devouring and destroying the United States. The nation barely knows that it is fighting for its life on simultaneous multiple fronts. All of these wars are being fought separately instead of seamlessly. Our elected leaders seem to ignore that the multiple integrated threats we face are but facets of a many-sided menace. Instead, we treat them as separate unrelated challenges.

US economic growth has hovered at one to two percent annually during most of the twenty-first century. Just as good fiscal policy and governance were returning growth to a range of two to four percent, COVID-19 acid washed the economy into contraction. Thus, our economic wherewithal to muster defense and countermeasures was substantially eroded.

At the same time, the Constitution has suffered systematic undermining from within, especially in the era of COVID-19. Response to the health emergency has justified a gamut of patchworked local emergency decrees and invasions of personal rights, often dispensing with due process, often resembling a decree-based authoritarian state.

With menacing synchrony, the US is now threatened by the very enemies that our country's past leaderships worked hard to appease. As we roll out one defense measure and reaction after another, America's enemies have not hesitated to accelerate their attacks or plot them on the world's chessboard. During the profusion of multifront threats in 2020, the Trump administration has failed to formulate a comprehensive and integrated global or domestic strategy to save us.

How did we get here?

The Obama administration strangled economic growth from 2008 to 2016. For those eight years, the government targeted the banking system by levying fines on banks of nearly $150 billion because they had complied with various federal home ownership laws and regulations passed since 1992. Those laws and regulations compelled loaning money to high-risk home buyers, a practice which eventually collapsed the real estate market. Further attacks on the banks were channeled through excessive Dodd-Frank Act regulations. Those regulations, many arbitrarily and poorly thought out, kneecapped bank profitability. Corroded profits multiplied merger madness spurred on by federal mandates or market necessity. Thus, healthy institutions were injected with toxic or declining organizations that were damaged by the expensive regulation and poor management that ignited the process.

Adding to the banking disaster was a massive attempt to nationalize the health insurance industry and thereby control the American people through President Obama's Affordable Care Act (ACA), often derided as "The Unaffordable Care Act." Many saw this hodge-podge of policy overreaches as redistribution of economic resources masquerading as vast and sorely needed improvement in healthcare delivery. As it robbed most people of affordable healthcare, it triggered a spiraling rise in costs facing insurance companies, providers, and industry professionals, who gamed the system with unconscionable price escalation and selective market abandonment.

Trebling down on its destructive policies, the Obama administration also attacked the coal and the natural gas fracking industries through more onerous Environmental Protection Agency (EPA) regulations, with unionized companies receiving rough handling by the National Labor Relations Board (NLRB). While this undermining was underway, corporate investors were battered by an excessive 35 percent tax rate, the highest in the industrialized world. The economic warfare waged on the private sector resulted in an abysmal, sub-par economic recovery of only one to two percent growth from the Bush-era recession, triggered by the 2008–2009 financial crisis.

Every deleterious economic impact that has struck the system has been worsened by a public education and university system that sadly impairs and subverts rather than elevates our culture. The Bush administration's "No Child Left Behind" program might have been well-intentioned, but it forced the Federal government into local school oversight. The Obama government further imposed its own local education policy by threatening to cut their federal funding. To be specific, the Obama administration imposed the Federal Common Core Curriculum to foster false narratives about US history, its laws, free speech, civics, socialism, climate change, identity politics, religion, and political Islam. Regarding grades K–12, the government deprived parents and children of school choice through a scarcity of voucher programs and insufficient numbers of charter schools. On the cultural front, the Obama administration promoted political correctness and victimhood as well as attacks on Judeo-Christian values through the ACA's birth control mandates and so-called "transgender bathrooms." All these self-wounding policies were aided and abetted by academia and co-opted major media outlets. Obama's foreign and domestic policies combined corrosively to leave us at the precipice of World War III, yet without a strategy for defense or victory.

The radical Islamic threat began in 1928, when the Muslim Brotherhood was born in Egypt to promote Islam as a political movement, determined to challenge and replace Western civilization. The first successful Islamic revolution since WWI took root when a Muslim theocracy seized power in Iran in 1979. Iran openly declared war on America when it captured the US Embassy in Tehran. The success of the Islamic Republic of Iran showed the vulnerability of America. The Islamist notion of "civilization jihad" is a pre-violent tactic deployed against infidels, those who disbelieve the tenets of Islam. This form of jihad has achieved different stages of success across the world. Even now, continuous attacks in various countries are launched by al-Qaeda, ISIS, the Muslim Brotherhood and its proxies, and their Iranian counterparts.

Iran was decisively secured in the driver's seat of the Islamic revolution by the Obama administration with the Joint Comprehensive Plan of Action (JCPOA), which facilitated the mullahs' nuclear weapons agenda. As a consequence of the JCPOA, it was granted the right to produce nuclear weapons by 2025 even as it furiously continued development of ICBMs. In the process, Iran was provided $150 billion by the Obama administration to finance that nuclear program, thereby bypassing the Nuclear Proliferation Treaty through its heretofore illegal nuclear development activities.

How do we meet our key converging challenges? The US must focus on re-emphasizing its traditional values of "Life, Liberty, and the pursuit of Happiness." Here is the three-pronged outline:

A. "Life" means "Enhancing US national security":
   1. Stop the nuclear programs that are fast advancing in Iran and North Korea.
   2. Countercheck Iran's penetration of Latin America and Africa.
   3. Increase defense and related spending at least five percent annually; upgrade cyber offense/defense as well as cultural war strategies.
   4. Defend our energy infrastructure and electrical grid.
   5. Regain control over borders and immigration.
   6. Replace the UN with a "Covenant of Democratic Nations." (Private initiatives have failed, and the effort can only succeed with US governmental action.)

B. "Liberty" means "Protecting and reviving Judeo-Christian values":
   1. Promote individual liberties as well as states' rights as they comply with the US Constitution.

2. Enact legislation precluding any admission of Sharia principles into the US juridical system.
3. Reform the entire educational system, ensuring that Western values survive while expanding school choice.
4. Ensure election integrity and guard against gerrymandering and hurriedly-implemented mass mail balloting.
5. Protect religious liberty in the US and worldwide.

C. "Happiness" means "Maximizing economic growth":
1. Repeal and replace the ACA/Obamacare and its individual mandate.
2. Reform all major entitlement programs.
3. Stop intergenerational confiscatory taxing.
4. Reform national energy policy, maximizing production.
5. Enact right-to-work statutes in every state.

Currently, the US and the entire western world are failing on all three of these defense vectors. When the US finally executes strategies that succeed on all three platforms, its citizens, the country, and all of Western civilization will be strengthened. These three challenges are the building blocks of any successful society. For good reason, our Declaration of Independence exalted the phrase "Life, Liberty, and the pursuit of Happiness."

Our current defense ineptitude calls for a new, invigorated all-encompassing, always-adapting master plan. In 1982–1984, President Ronald Reagan devised a strategy to defeat the Soviet Union that drew upon economics, military development, science, and diplomacy. The fragmented, non-integrated strategy now bubbling up will never deter our enemies. No one can deny that our plans must constantly recalibrate due to the battle with COVID-19.

But careful refocus, intrepid clarity, and galvanized comprehension can defeat our adversaries and save our civilization, which is now being assaulted in a multifront war.

Chapter Two: False Narratives

America and most of the Western world are misled by both radical progressive Left and Islamist false narratives. We can easily speculate that during the time of Abraham—3,800 years ago, 99 percent of the world's population believed in idols and many gods. Judeo-Christian philosophy and religions began replacing idols and polytheism 3,800 years ago, and it took fifteen more centuries for the concept to flower. Monotheism as espoused by the major Abrahamic religions sanctified the concept of individual equality and morality, establishing a code of good and evil—howsoever imperfect—which has constantly tried to bring the harsh realities of human nature to the loftier values of the belief system.

The concept of liberty itself was born during the famous Exodus of the Israelites. It is expressed as a mandamus in the third book of Moses, Leviticus. In Chapter 25:10, the Israelites are commanded, "Go forth and proclaim liberty throughout the land to all its inhabitants." More than three millennia passed before American colonists established their revolutionary form of self-government, which enshrined that ancient commandment to achieve human liberty. So inherent to the American enterprise were the words of Leviticus 25:10 that the phrase is emblazoned on the Liberty Bell. The yearning to achieve equality flowered into our current American democracy. As a human undertaking, America's progress has been continual, and the circle of entitlement and democratic inclusion has grown larger with each generation.

History has proven that America's effort was immensely flawed at first because it labored under evils inherited from Europe. But the American experiment—which from its outset embarked upon "a more perfect union"—demarcated a turning point moment in human history. Our ability to reform for the sake of individual freedom is an exceptional achievement in the story of human society. Our cycle of improvement and betterment has given rise to the very concept of "American exceptionalism."

But now, American exceptionalism is under attack from the proliferation and dominance of false narratives, often led by so-called progressives. In many ways, Progressives are actually *regressives*, who want to take us back into a time when kings and other dictators made decisions for all subjects under their control. Core American values of life, liberty, the pursuit of happiness, freedom of speech, equal opportunity, and "One Nation Under God," howsoever imperfect, are under attack by progressives.

Unfortunately, many Americans now have trouble remembering and recognizing such exceptionalism—an achievement that took some 3,800 years to develop. America is still struggling to become more inclusive, to fulfill its original ideal. We see this in the roiling wake of 2020's twin historic challenges—the response to COVID-19 and the searing aftermath of the televised murder of George Floyd, an American of African descent. Our ability to demand improvement of ourselves is salient proof of our exceptionalism. But those improvements must adhere to our democratic principles. Democratic changes as a society are, in fact, what makes these changes improvements—not impositions.

Progressives today strive to erode or subdue our democracy. Their central tactic depends upon four major false narratives, aided by their fellow travelers in the press. Absent press co-option, these destructive notions could never take root. But the Pravdaization of the American media has allowed false narratives to magnify to the level of a major threat to our way of life.

The first false narrative is perpetrated by a convergence of radical leftists, progressives, socialists, and communists. For them, dictating their version of equality is the key to salvation. In their world, deified government ensures that hand-selected authoritarian overlords determine and enforce social, economic, political, and individual conduct. This whole concept inherently denies individual freedoms and the core of democratic values, which require "the consent of the governed."

In the false narrative that promotes the ascendance of an all-dominating government, "God-given rights" are replaced with "government-permitted rights." Yet, America has witnessed that, as the role of federal government control over the economy grows by virtue of excessive proliferation of regulations and prohibitions—not to mention the inherent corruption of such dominating systems, economic investment and growth slow. Enlarged government shrinks economic vitality as it crushes. Under such a regime, the oxygen of prosperity is systematically sucked out of the political ecosystem. This false narrative of the Left always leads to economic deterioration of all segments of the population except, of course, for the ruling class and its chosen political party. Inevitably, engorged government concentrates its power into a small circle of corrupt hands. The very term "ruling class" owes its existence to such totalitarian systems.

The fate of false narratives in power politics was shown vividly to the world in 1989 with the fall of the Berlin Wall and the mass migrations to the West. Unfortunately, no trials took place to force former Soviet leaders to pay for their crimes, as took place in Nuremberg after the defeat of Germany and Nazism in 1945. Approximately 60 million people were killed in WWII, and the Allied victors insisted on German de-Nazification. During the period from 1917 to 1989, Russian leaders killed an estimated 30 million of their own people through direct execution or, indirectly through economic mismanagement and starvation. Meanwhile, the Soviet Union transformed itself into an economically-oriented competitor as well as a purely military antagonist.

The false lure of communism (direct government and single-party control over corporations) along with its sister ideology, socialism (which trumpets pseudo-benign government control) is once more alive and well. Today, these two ideologies continue to prosper in the US and Europe, infecting our educational systems. Universities now pride themselves over the diversity of their student body and professional ranks. But look again. Diversity in their handbook is based on race, geography, and gender, yet purposely ignores the far more important and relevant ideological basis for the diversity of ideas. Therefore, it is not uncommon for the overwhelming majority of typical humanities departments to be staffed by professors hostile to the US, our Constitution, and other traditional beliefs that create America's unique way of life. The concept of intersectionality relies upon the controlled convergence of strategies from divergent groups to serve a singular cause.

Many hostile and alien ideologies were imported from the Frankfurt School, the school of thought created by German Marxists in the 1930s to create a cultural reformation that fought for such notions as absolute idealism. The Frankfurt School employed Freudian idealism to sharpen the tactics of nineteenth-century classical Marxism in the twentieth century. It integrated strains of anti-positivist sociology, psycho-analysis, and existentialism to achieve its political goals. While such notions as absolute idealism may seem to be grist for philosophers and abstract thinkers, this type of logic assault became an active tactic among those determined to foist their notions on others and change our society to conform to their twisted vision.

Frankfurt School pseudo-intellectuals and their devotees sought to undermine the family and the father figure in favor of international Marxism or multiculturalism. More familiarly, Frankfurt School practitioners proliferated "political correctness" to shut down legitimate debate, thus limiting free speech and any intellectual impediment to their seizure of power.

True, students of the Frankfurt School of thought control may not even know they are enrolled. However, adherents to Frankfurt School dogma—whether or not they realize the roots of such thinking—can be found in the most important opinion-making sectors of our society.

The mass media and entertainment industries are chief among those promoting this false narrative. These entities regularly demean hardworking businessmen and basic American free market values, while extolling so-called "social justice" values and the importance of a strong government. In this conversation, terrorism and Islamism—political Islam—are rarely addressed or honestly discussed. Despite the endless roster of action films produced in Hollywood, the glitterati display a basic tolerance of political Islam, which itself is a false narrative. Here, the politicization of a religion seeks to replace our Constitution with Sharia, derived from a long-obsolete morality which arose among Arabs in the desert 1,400 years ago. Yet, in this always-playing, slow-motion, and never-ending movie, America is often portrayed as a villain and rarely for what it is: an exceptional country that lionizes individual freedoms, with superior economic growth and a common culture of hard work and honesty, accessible to all. It is only because our society elevates individual freedoms that historical injustices imported from Europe and the Arabian Peninsula can be periodically addressed and rectified. Further proof of the inherent power of our democracy to heal our own historical injustices is realized in changes, both incremental and radical, that have been adopted.

To be sure, American society and history have overflowed with sad examples of outrageous behavior, systemic prejudice, and stifling injustice. But our exceptional ability to spotlight injustice in our midst and reform—a perpetual task for any complex society—

only bolsters the inherent exceptionalism of our nation. In many other societies, such as China and the Islamic world, discord, injustice, and repression of the individual are cemented features. The very nature of such societies empowers them to eradicate individual challenges to maintain things the way they have been and prevent change. For example, despite all the protest and tumult in effervescent Hong Kong, that territory has now being swallowed back into the repressive grip of the Chinese Communist Party. In Saudi Arabia, women have only recently been permitted to drive automobiles, machines invented at the end of the nineteenth century and introduced into the peninsula more than a century ago. In Russia, troublesome journalists are murdered or disappear—that is, not in Stalinist Russia, but in today's Putinesque realm.

As part of the homegrown ideological campaign against America, we see a gilded tolerance for the disintegration of the family unit. This can only be achieved by perforating religious institutions and communities. The so-called "opiate of the people" postulated by Karl Marx is more fully grasped by a longer quotation of his writing:

> "Religious suffering is, at one and the same time, the expression of real suffering and a protest against real suffering. Religion is the sigh of the oppressed creature, the heart of a heartless world, and the soul of soulless conditions. It is the opiate of the people. The abolition of religion as the illusory happiness of the people is the demand for their real happiness."

The erosion of our norms produces family units where nearly 40 percent of all children are born out of wedlock. That number rises to 60 percent for Hispanics and about 75 percent for Blacks. The breakdown of the family in general and the reduced presence of the father in particular inflict huge social and economic problems on the children.

Fatherless families yield cyclical disadvantages, especially among minorities. Without a father present, mothers are often stopped in their education to tend to the child, and then accept a stunted job path that fluctuates around permanent entry-level status. Grandparents are brought in to raise the child. Economic disadvantage is passed from generation to generation. With economic disadvantage comes bad neighborhoods, bad schools, bad policing, and broken families trapped by their own limitations. This legacy becomes destiny for youngsters, who in turn replicate these experiences. Thus, we see the generation-to-generation affliction of poverty, inequality, and disadvantage spin on inexorably.

The broken family syndrome is intensified by illicit drugs from Latin America and the Middle East pouring through the southern border. Controlling that despicable trade is a collage of narco-terrorist groups, Iranian operators, and remnant ISIS factions or analogous organizations. Marijuana is being legitimized by many states for so-called "medicinal" purposes and even recreational use in some states, such as Colorado. Yet, in the absence of long-term clinical trials, as required by the Food and Drug Administration (FDA) for all new pharmaceuticals, this gateway drug has become a way of life for too many. During the 2020 COVID-19 lockdowns, churches were forced to close, but marijuana shops were deemed essential and allowed to stay open. Pastors were arrested for holding religious services, but protest gatherings after the George Floyd murder were encouraged by government officials.

Clearly, the progressive movement—socialists or the radical Left—has taken control of much of the media, entertainment, and educational systems. This progressive movement is really a reactionary Marxist movement dedicated to reversing the 3,800-year journey behind the rise of individual rights and personal responsibility.

Free thought itself has been lassoed and restrained by a series of progressive manifestoes. The first successful progressive project in the US that sought to legislate personal behavior was the Eighteenth Amendment—Prohibition—which went into effect in 1920. The entire Prohibition era ended as a dismal failure. Despite the debacle of Prohibition, this was only the beginning for the social control brigades.

More Federal government programs aimed at reshaping and controlling our society have emerged over the decades. A prime example is the Common Core curriculum, which actually undermines traditional American values in education and family life. As in Muslim madrassas, American children subjected to Common Core are increasingly taught to recite instead of to analyze and think.

The plethora of similar projects are often buttressed by well-financed non-governmental organizations (NGOs), funded by various millionaire businessmen or their foundations, financing hundreds of anti-

American organizations in both the US and abroad. Interestingly, these organizations almost always maintain charitable tax exemptions, but are clearly political organizations that do not warrant such status. Yet, the US Treasury Department and American legislation does nothing to change this false status.

The Affordable Care Act (ACA), also known as Obamacare, is another vivid example of a false narrative at work. It promised individual health care choice, but delivered government-imposed mediocrity. In practice, citizens often had to switch health insurance plans and their physician providers. Somehow—inexplicably—the ACA was broadened beyond healthcare, nationalizing the country's student loan program. The Health Care and Education Reconciliation Act, passed after the ACA, was designed to amend the ACA and subsume the loan program into a health care administrative octopus. Clearly, student loans are unrelated to health care. Nationalizing them in the ACA constituted a clear federal government power grab.

Worse, challenges to the ACA were illicitly repressed, as President Obama's administration itself became lawless. A weaponized Internal Revenue Service (IRS) attacked thousands of conservative not-for-profits by taking away or otherwise subverting their tax-exempt status without due process during the 2012–2016 period. Other instances abound.

Without Congressional authorization or approval, the US agreed in 2016 to hand over control of the Internet to an unaccountable organization called the Internet Corporation of Assigned Names and Numbers (ICANN). ICANN is a one-world supranational but unelected entity that controls our individual lives. In fact, its motto is "One World. One Internet." Whether or not they do a good or needed job is not the issue. ICANN controls much of our daily lives and our ability to express ourselves freely. Yet no one elected them, and they answer only to themselves.

Another example of regulatory overreach can be seen in the recent behavior of major governmental departments that operate directly under presidential authority, such as the Environmental Protection Agency (EPA), Housing and Urban Development (HUD), Department of Education, the Treasury Department, and the heretofore totally unaccountable Consumer Financial Protection Board (which has done nothing discernible to actually protect consumers). This never-elected and often unaccountable governance is understandably referred to as "the fourth branch of government."

Infringement of the American right to approve those who govern us and consent to governance has plugged neatly into a globalized trend of transnational organizations such as the United Nations (UN) and regional organizations like the European Union (EU), which trample on the rights of sovereign countries and their citizens.

The UN arose in the last days of 1941, after the bombing of Pearl Harbor, when two democratic WWII allies, Great Britain and the United States, agreed with Mao's civil war-torn China and Stalin's Soviet Union to form the organization. The bargain with two totalitarian regimes was not to assure democracy, but to ensure full Russian participation in the war against the Axis—that is, not only against Germany, but also Japan, which had bombed Hawaii a few weeks earlier. How could the UN be a guarantor of human rights and democracy when its dominant founders included two nations who did not believe in individual freedoms or liberties? Despite the later inclusion of more democracies, such as liberated France, greater growth occurred among the blocs of non-democratic and freedom-abhorring nations.

The European Union arose from a legitimized coal and steel cartel, which tried to fix and control coal prices—much like the Organization of the Petroleum Exporting Countries (OPEC). Even though the European Coal and Steel Community (ECSC) claimed it had created the world's first anti-cartel agency, that was done to avoid any effort to stymie its price-fixing supranationalism. Later, the ECSC expanded its list of price-fixed and controlled goods, thereby creating the Common Market, and subsequently expanded its commercial controls into civilian controls. This in turn gave rise to the European Union. These supranational organizations promulgate the chief false narratives of our day.

Such supranational control entities espouse key false narratives of government-loving leftists, global government exponents, and selective isolationists, all in league with Islamists. In Europe, the EU's European Parliament has replaced the sovereign decision-making of its member countries. Britain finally rebelled with Brexit, reclaiming its own sovereignty. Other member states continue to debate whether they shall emulate Great Britain's departure.

Moreover, in the UN Security Council, such enemies of democracy as Russia and China wield veto rights over American national security. Worse, within the General Assembly, the 56 Muslim countries in the Organization of Islamic Cooperation (OIC) represent about thirty percent of the 193 UN member countries, and consistently vote as a block against Western countries and values.

President Donald Trump has vowed to cut funding to the UN and reform it, but this reform is still in its infancy. A small step in that direction has been the defunding of the World Health Organization (WHO), which, during the 2020 COVID-19 pandemic, proved a font of false information, flipping its recommendations and cautions like a loose light switch.

Both the UN and the EU personify the false narratives of world and regional organizations that seek globalization. Their only sometimes hidden mantra calls for a "world without borders," and therefore, one without distinct identified cultures and territorial security. The false narrative of these worldwide and regional organizations leads to the weakening of formerly strong nation-states and to the economic, cultural, and military detriment of each individual country that cherishes individual liberties.

The ideologies behind isolationists and libertarians propel the argument against involvement in foreign wars, even when justified and compelling. Such self-locking naivety assumes that bad actors abroad will stay in their own countries. Unfortunately, isolationism encourages the forces of evil to gain regional domination. From that hegemony, they extend their reach across the world—even to our shores. Therefore, fewer entanglements abroad lead to increased danger at home. George Washington's 1796 farewell address, in which he encouraged us to avoid foreign entanglements, was promulgated at a time when great oceans secured us and no airplanes threatened us. This is not the case today.

Most Americans still feel that they are protected by the vast oceans that hug our shores and friendly relations with Canada and Mexico that buffer us to the north and south. We are seemingly surrounded by safety. These Americans generally do not support higher levels of military expenditures, nor US military actions abroad, nor foreign military assistance to our allies. Sadly, every other democratic country also has its group of isolationists, who focus on their short-term, narrow definition of "self-interest" to the detriment of their own long-term interests and security.

Dictators of Islamist countries inevitably promote the most dangerous false narratives, so false that their ideology must be forcibly imposed on their own populations. Dissent is not tolerated by such governments. The people are compelled to jettison free thought, both political and economic. As expected, economic growth is stifled under such regimes. Invariably, all segments of the population suffer except, of course, the ruling class.

Intellectually armed with false narratives, worldwide political Islamic terror organizations and countries have declared war on the US and Western civilization. Collectively, five terror entities pose an existential threat to the US: Iran, the Muslim Brotherhood (MB), the so-called Islamic State (ISIS), al-

Qaeda, and the Wahhabi religious cult (historically supported by Saudi Arabia and many of the Gulf States).

These Islamic terror groups have declared war on Western Civilization—and each other. For example, Iran and Syria are fighting ISIS in Syria and Iraq. Saudi Arabia is challenging the Sunni Muslim Brotherhood (Turkey and Qatar) and Shiite Iran. The Taliban (supported in varying degrees by Pakistan, Saudi Arabia, Russia, and even Iran) are fighting ISIS in Afghanistan as well as the official central government there. Hence, to protect itself, the US must systematically struggle with all these physical and cultural terror entities in a simultaneous fashion, taking care to ensure that the defeat of any single one of them does not merely serve to strengthen the others.

Drilling down into the ideological tactics of our adversaries, we find their toolkits contain a long roster of false sub-narratives. For example, big government advocates claim that redistribution of wealth will aid 90 percent of society. In truth, redistribution of wealth hurts 100 percent of the population. "One-worlders" argue that even bigger worldwide supragovernments, such as the European Union, are capable of better management of the affairs of individual countries than those countries themselves. But democratically elected and managed nations always superintend their affairs better when they can respond to local constituencies. Isolationists claim the oceans and mountains will protect us from terrorists. In truth, terrorists will cross the oceans, traverse the mountains, and find us wherever we are.

An entire cadre of false narratives about militant or political Islam cannot help conflating the bloodlust of entities such as ISIS and al-Qaeda with the legitimate manifestation of the peaceful movements of Islam. In truth, Islamism seeks to conquer, destroy, or subjugate those who do not abandon their own religious upbringing and convert. Beginning in the 1920s, the religion of Islam has been taken hostage by the revival of dangerous Islamic movements every bit as dangerous as other historically false narrative authoritarian movements, such as communism, fascism, and Japanese imperialism. Appeasement did not stem the outrages of Nazism and will not even dampen the threat of militant Islam.

Indeed, militant Islam often targets its own coreligionists first. The same core danger applies to the Palestinian Authority (PA) in its peace process prestidigitation. The PA does not seek to coexist with Israel nor to allow Jews to exist within its midst. The Oslo Accords—now reduced to a figment of withered, weathered, and ambiguously drafted text—are just a means to an end. Both Oslo I and Oslo II, along with their various adjunct agreements, have been abrogated, violated, or terminated by the PA itself. The PA's main goal is to periodically use the Oslo Accords as just another ill-tempered tactic to fetch big dollars from the international community.

NATO, on its surface, seems like a sensible common defense pact between the United States and its European allies. However, when European nations spend only one to two percent of their own GDP on national defense, they cannot or will not protect their own people, leaving it the United States to shoulder the effort. This will only further embroil us in war. In other words, a weak or weakened defense encourages offensive acts against us.

Another dangerous sub-narrative swirls around Iran, asserting that Iran is a country run by rational actors seeking proper and respectful integration into the world community. In fact, the good people of Iran are now gripped by a professional terror organization seeking world domination. Iran stands as the world's leading sponsor of state terrorism.

More alternative universes are created by the false sub-narratives thrust upon us. One such narrative falsely claims that Israel treats Arabs as second-class citizens; when, in fact, the country's Arab constituency comprises 20 percent of the nation, and its political parties maintain a pivotal 15 percent grip on many state functions. A leading member of the Israeli Supreme Court hails from the Arab community. Arabs in Israel have far more rights than in any Arab nation. The aptly named Abraham Accord, signed by Israel with the UAE and with Bahrain, openly exposes the lie that peace is not possible in the Middle East unless the Palestinians orchestrate it.

A second narrative claims that the so-called "Arab Spring" was just a Muslim reformation surging into the modern world. In those countries where the Arab Spring erupted, we find the same intolerant relics of earlier generations; while, in the Gulf Arab nations, where the Arab Spring was mainly absent, many green shoots of modernity and peaceful coexistence are now regularly seen. Honest examination reveals the true season of discontent. Arab states such as Libya and Syria are moving further away from modernity in a sort of "Muslim Winter."

A third falsity swells up from the global warming debate. This multipart drama insists that taxes on high carbon emissions are needed to curb energy consumption to save the planet. High energy taxes are just an excuse for socialist governments to steal money from the people for redistribution to those the ruling class can control.

A fourth rallying cry weaponizes the term Islamophobia. On its face, Islamophobia is an irrational fear, racist dislike, or prejudice against Muslims. But a normal and logical fear of lslamists and jihadists—not of Muslims—is an understandable consequence of the jihadi war now being waged against civilized society. The two should not be confused.

Another deluding, false sub-narrative assures the world that the US, as the world's great superpower, will protect the world with its cavalry. For his entire term, President Barack Obama was rapidly racing toward emulating the European process of self-induced national suicide. As a result, an internally divided, politically halved, and racially tone-deaf America may soon become a totally unreliable ally to its friends—and even to itself.

Discerning the threats and the connections among them is an immense challenge precisely because our senses are flooded with false narratives. Only by clear thinking and visual acuity can we see through the mirages and shiny distractions to perceive that each of our threats is but one facet of a multifront war.

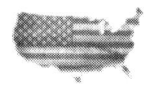

Chapter Three: The Islamist Hydra

Several major Islamist terror movements converge to create an Islamist hydra that threatens the United States—and all the world.

First among the surging heads of this monster is the Islamic Republic of Iran, which runs the most dangerous terror entity in the world today. The US Department of State officially calls Iran the "number one state sponsor of terrorism." The Iranian theocracy pretends to be a legitimate government. However, it is a theocratic terror regime promising to kill everyone in America (chanting "Death to America") and everyone in Israel (chanting "Death to Israel")—and indeed death to any Iranian within its national grasp who opposes it. The US is labeled the "Great Satan," and Israel the "Little Satan." Despite the sound and fury from Washington, the US government has no known strategy to stop or defeat Iran, other than applying medium pressure and calling it maximum.

Certainly, Iran is trying to take over the Middle East. Russia is actively helping, as is China.

The Iranian Shiites enjoy a historically anchored connection to Iraq's substantial Shia community, which has allowed Tehran to dominate Baghdad politically and play spoiler in all its national policies. Leading Iraqi mullahs, militiamen, and legislators get their marching orders as well as their monetary rewards from Tehran.

In Lebanon, Iran's Foreign Ministry funds and controls Hezbollah to control that country and foment constant war with Israel. Hezbollah has triggered almost all the Lebanese wars with Israel after the departure of the Palestine Liberation Organization (PLO) from the border lands. The group's name comes from the Arabic term for "The Party of God." Despite being declared a terrorist entity in the US as well as many parts of Europe and the Middle East, Hezbollah has managed to cement itself into Lebanon's governing coalition, thus derailing the country's every effort to rebuild itself as a peaceful, multiethnic nation. The gigantic August 2020 Beirut port explosion that obliterated so much of that city was, in fact, caused by 2,750 pounds of ammonium nitrate that had been stored by Hezbollah for years in case it was needed for truck bombs or other terrorist purposes.

In Syria, Iran was a pivotal ally of murderous dictator Bashar al-Assad. With his permission, Iran created an open and advertised military threat on Israel's border. Highly developed installations for ground forces and air assets were constructed, featuring advance shock troops from the Quds Forces. The stated goal was to invade Israel's north, seize and occupy northern towns, and even establish its own foreign administration on Israeli territory. Not until May 2020, after a withering Israeli bombing of its installations did Iranian forces temporarily pull back from the border. But from their point of view, they now have a direct military path from hostile Iranian territory to the Israeli fence.

More than a being a threat to its regional neighbors, Iran is also working to destabilize and hegemonize the whole world. Tehran is working closely with North

Korea on nuclear weapons and ICBM delivery systems. Simultaneously, the country is working across Latin America, where it has assembled and/or deeply ingrained itself into the largest narco-terror network in modern history. At the same time in Latin America, Iran runs the planet's largest Muslim terror-linked cultural organization through eighty cultural centers and broadcast stations. The widely distributed HispanTV does in many Latin American countries what PressTV does in the United States—it dispenses soft and hard propaganda. Iran also controls seventeen branches of Al-Mustafa University throughout Africa.

The Iranian Nuclear Deal, formally known as the Joint Comprehensive Plan of Action (JCPOA) has robustly financed Tehran's world designs. The P5+1 (US, England, France, Russia, China, plus Germany) negotiated poorly, and this succession of diplomatic and military errors bears an eerie resemblance to the world's inadequate response to the rise of Hitler and the false narrative of Nazism during the 1930s. Those errors led directly to World War II and to some sixty million casualties.

The second and ideological head of the Hydra is the Muslim Brotherhood (MB), founded by Hassan el-Bana in Egypt in 1928. El-Bana and his associate, Sayyid Qutb, established their political movement based on Islamism, or political Islam, which has been subsequently adopted by most radical and/or terrorist Islamic groups. The MB ranks as the number key cultural terror organization today in terms of its immediate danger to America and all of Western civilization. Primarily funded by Qatar, Turkey, and many other followers and business leaders around the world, the movement perches at the pinnacle of political Islam—Islamism.

In contrast to physical terror entities like Iran and ISIS, the MB mostly focuses on calculated deception through academia, the media, and NGOs. The MB intimidates its adversaries in democratic societies by employing political correctness and ill-considered court decisions within the very democracies it seeks to subvert. It also uses threats and implied violence to back up its "requests" in the Islamic world. Among the leading methods in its toolkit are demographic warfare, waged by promoting multiple marriages among its adherents—regardless of whether the society permits multiple marriages. In the US and Canada alone, the MB operates through several dozen front organizations, many already identified in various court documents.

Further obscuring the attack lines, two major and distinct MB branches are operating in the US today, one based in Egypt and one in Pakistan. The previous Bush and Obama administrations actually supported the MB. The Trump administration has yet to recognize the threat or to define a new strategy to defeat it. Though Washington has devised a strategy to physically defeat ISIS, al-Qaeda Takfiri, and Salafi forces on the ground, we have yet to devise a mechanism to defeat Islamists ideologically and culturally while they remain in their pre-military stages.

ISIS and al-Qaeda, the third head of the Hydra, make no effort to conceal their intent. Despite their well-known defeats on the ground, both terrorist organizations are actively implementing an agenda for further territorial domination. These global movements had set up caliphates in Syria and Iraq, in Africa, and among the Taliban in Afghanistan—but those territorial realms have largely been dismantled. Yet this third most threatening entity would rise to the top again if it possessed the resources of Iran or the MB. Nonetheless, even after its territorial decimation in Syria and Iraq, ISIS and al Qaeda forces continue to organize and incite terror attacks by both their members and "lone wolves" throughout Europe, Africa, and the US. It is true that the commanders dispatch their terror from numerous bases in the Middle East and Africa. But no place in the Westernized world is safe from these attacks.

Security experts begrudgingly admit that previous US administrations were complicit in the rise of ISIS and adopted no coherent strategy to defeat it. In essence, the Islamic State filled the void that was created by the Obama administration after its purposely precipitous withdrawal of American troops from Iraq in 2012. Moreover, when ISIS attacked Iraqi warehouses filled with $4 billion worth of American equipment, the Obama administration did nothing to blow up this stolen property before it could be redeployed by ISIS, thereby, in effect, arming ISIS. We are fighting a force armed with our own weapons.

The fourth head of the Hydra is the Wahhabi movement itself. Wahhabism originated in Saudi Arabia but has by now spread to other Muslim countries—especially Pakistan. It imposes draconian Islamic law through the use of the police forces and legal courts that it dominates. Working together, the Wahhabis and MB support an estimated eighty percent of the 3,000 mosques in the US with foreign financing and the importation of foreign-trained imams and the establishment of schools. This follows Saudi Arabia's strategic 1960s decision to fund the expansion of mosques throughout the Western world. Saudi Arabia and Gulf States such as Qatar also finance Middle East Studies departments in more than ten major universities and subsidize many of the nearly 100,000 Muslim students studying in US universities. Additional financing comes from Turkey and Iran, both of which have their long arms deep in American university departments. These Islamist financial streams are augmented by European governments long complicit in the rise of Islamism—witness EU financing for Islamist mosque construction and even NGOs acting as fronts for such terrorist groups as the Popular Front for the Liberation of Palestine.

It is important to recognize that 2019 and 2020 events in Saudi Arabia could signal the onset of a major change. The May 2017 visit by President Trump seems to have triggered the beginnings of a tectonic change of the Kingdom's socio-political landscape. Saudi Arabia is, as of this writing, led by Crown Prince Mohammed bin Salman, known by the affectionate acronym "MBS." He has begun a hopefully unstoppable movement to diversify the economy, curb outdated Wahhabi beliefs, reclaim Islam from the Islamists, and reintroduce personal freedoms. MBS is also encouraging improved security relations with Israel, though these are still out of public view. Unfortunately, the December 2019 terror attack by a Saudi student at Naval Air Station Pensacola in Florida shows that the Saudi reform effort is still in its early stages. A single gunman can set progress back. America should do everything possible to encourage promising changes by MBS and allied Saudi forces for modernization.

Regardless of improvements in Saudi Arabia, our ability to confront the hydra of political Islam is made all the more difficult by the insidious use of *taqiyya*, the purposeful Islamic strategy of dissimulation or outright lying to enemies. Sharia endorses lies and deception to help Islamists deceive infidels and hide their strategic goals, such as taking over host countries. The concept of taqiyya is often said to arise from the Quranic injunction found in Sura 3:28: "Let not the believers take the unbelievers for friends rather than believers; and whoever does this, he shall have nothing of (the guardianship of) Allah, but you should guard yourselves against them, guarding carefully; and Allah makes you cautious of (retribution from) Himself; and to Allah is the eventual coming." Several of the key Arabic words in the phrase derive from taqiyya, which connotes *prudence* and *fear*.

Scholars can argue the intent of Sura 3:28, but in practice, Islamists rely upon the taqiyya concept to deviously claim Islamophobia to silence legitimate criticism. Noted fourteenth-century Islamic historian Ibn Kathir explained, "In some areas or times, [Muslims] fear for their safety from the disbelievers. In this case, such believers are allowed to show friendship to the disbelievers outwardly, but never inwardly." The Prophet Muhammad's companion, Abu Ad-Darda', averred, "We smile in the face of some people although our hearts curse them." The tactical use of taqiyya, according to al-Hasan, is neither temporary nor solely for exigent circumstances, but "is acceptable till the Day of Resurrection."

The four terror heads of the hydra carry out physical war, intellectual war, cultural war, economic war, legal war, and demographic war in their quest for world domination. Yet, the US has developed no strategy to identify these simultaneous threats as part of a multifront onslaught. All of the West's current strategies are deficient.

On the military front, the Pentagon is not configured to simultaneously fight battles in twenty to forty theaters on top of two major regional wars. Domestically, the FBI and local police are not generally configured to identify terror cells and arrest the operatives before they commit terror attacks. Several undercover traps have been sprung against willing combatants before they could purchase weapons or genuine explosives. But preventive action is extremely hard to organize and outmatched by the volume of threats.

On the cultural front, because threats have not been identified, and because until now, the authorities have often relied on advice from Muslim Brotherhood operatives who have penetrated the government's security apparatus, we have no domestic or worldwide capacity to undermine and confront the false narratives disseminated by Islamist organizations.

On the economic front, our Treasury Department has not yet designated crippling sanctions on all four of the hydra terror entities or their affiliates. True, crippling sanctions have been levied against Iran by the Trump administration, but new ones are constantly introduced as Trump continues incremental intensifycation.

On the legal front, the power triad of the White House, the State Department, and the Justice Department has no cohesive plan or legal framework to continuously prosecute the four heads of the hydra, especially when it comes to seeking damages on behalf of their US victims. The Justice Department does not and cannot forbid the filing of frivolous lawsuits by these terror organizations. Such suits are all too often politicized as part an effort to increase domestic chaos.

On the demographic front, we maintain poor control over our borders. There are no government-run education programs or, better yet, government-financed vouchers that new immigrants must use to educate themselves about our way of life, civics, and Western values. Typically, first-wave immigrants try to bring in their families. In net, immigration laws rooted in a prior century have not been modernized to adjust to our current security challenges.

Our lack of preparedness and action plans enables Iran's partner North Korea to proceed unabated in its cyberattacks. It is more than North Korea. Too often we see Iranian interests simultaneously advanced by cyber assaults from China and Russia.

When we envision WWIII, the conflagration confronting us is essentially the third jihad waged by political Islam. The first jihad saw Islamism spread from the Middle East to Africa in the west and as far as Indonesia on the east (650–750 CE). The second Jihad brought the war to Europe and Russia (1300–1650 CE). The third jihad began in 1928 in Egypt and is now seeking world domination over all Christians, Hindus, and Jews. The 9/11 attacks were just a warm-up. The success or demise of this war will become obvious over the next fifty years. Either Western civilization or political Islam will survive.

For years, observers have delineated three stages which will manifest in a third jihad. First, Islamists will pretend to fit into a new society through taqiyya, purposefully concealing their true intentions. In the second stage, they will falsely portray themselves as victims. The third will be to offensively take over the host country, probably by embedding themselves in domestic unrest such as racial strife.

The US is in stage one now and moving into stage two. Within such European countries as France, Holland, Belgium and Sweden, stage three is already burning. Over the next fifty years, virtually all Western European countries where Muslims make up more than twenty percent of the population will probably find themselves in breakaway partition plans or civil wars, not unlike what India endured when Pakistan was cleaved from it, and not unlike the Islamic insurrection in the Philippines led by the Abu Sayyaf group. The exceptions to this rule will be Israel, India, China and Russia, each of which has learned how to manage its Muslim minorities.

The hydra organizations work strategically with local partners to destabilize and undermine American interests in Latin America and the Caribbean basin. This is currently achieved through at least ten main vectors. First, consider five state actors. 1) Iran's Republican Guard and its allies provide intel to our adversaries and gather intel about our relationships. Unconventional warfare against our interests is also part of their mission. 2) Russia's Federal Security Bureau (successor to the KGB) is in league with various

Russian intel and military assets, along with their function in the cyber, energy and nuclear sales spaces. 3) The People's Liberation Army of China penetrates cyberspace and engages in profound economic warfare. 4) Turkey, under President Recep Tayyip Erdoğan, engages in constant economic and political warfare while its government-allied commercial arms search for gold. 5) The Bolivarian Alliance of the Americas (ALBA) wields its "Troika of Tyranny," which works to spread socialism throughout the continent.

Add to these five national actors numerous non-state and quasi-state actors—each clearly identified and controlled by various adversary governments, which continue to wage war on the US and its allies. The list includes Russian and Iranian academic networks; Shia mosques and schools, financed through Iran's Al-Mustafa University; Sunni mosques, financed by Turkey and Saudi Arabia; Mexican, Colombian, and Central American transnational criminal organizations and gangs; and North Korean-controlled smuggling operations. Hence, in Latin America, we face a diversified but simultaneous assault of state-sponsored or state-controlled espionage, sabotage, terrorism, smuggling, and political subversion on our nation's southern flank.

While the hydra rages on our southern flank, it engages in similar operations in Africa and around the world. Understanding the combined forces against us is the first step toward readying a defense—albeit long overdue—for the multifront war.

Chapter Four: Israel's Success Story

Israel, as the source of Judaism, also represents the foundation and focal point of Western values. One often hears the phrase "Judeo-Christian values." This means that the ethical, juridical, and freedom precepts so prized today by democracies were almost all originally postulated in founding Jewish traditions, teachings, and texts, and later embraced by Christianity.

Israel is often regarded as the eastern frontier of American and Western civilization. Some refer to it as the West's aircraft carrier in the region. Yet, the Jewish state faces a continuous war for its very existence. The constellation of threats is mind-boggling, especially considering Israel's tiny size.

The hostile forces seem insurmountable. Count them: the Iranian regime; the Palestinian Authority (PA); relentless cyberwarfare teams; Iranian forces in Syria and Iraq; Hezbollah, poised in southern Lebanon and southern Syria; Iraqi militias armed with missiles; Hamas and the Palestinian Islamic Jihad armed with rockets; Bedouins in the Negev, who do not recognize any state's sovereignty; thousands of illegal African Muslim immigrants; nonstop threats to the country's offshore gas and oil fields; and well-armed remnants of ISIS roaming the Sinai and the Jordanian border realm. Add to these a confederation of governmental and academic haters ensconced in the United Nations; the

European Union; the recently-established International Criminal Court, with its disputed authority; and an acronymic soup of belligerent NGOs, all in league with hate-infused universities and media, eager to shore up any gaps in the encirclement. Israel's daily survival and ability to thrive is surely one of the miracles in Jewish history. For Israel, simple survival is victory. Ironically, with all the annihilation threats against it, the coffee shops, beaches, and clubs of Israel host a populace that consistently tells survey questioners that they live in one of the happiest places on Earth.

Although challenged to fight on multiple fronts, Israel has been fighting for its survival every day since its rebirth in 1948. In fact, Jews have been fighting to survive every day since Abraham's time, some 3,800 years ago, when Abraham declared polytheism to be a false narrative. His vision gave rise to the great Abrahamic religions—not only Judaism, Christianity, and Islam, but also later monotheistic variants. These evolved into the belief systems practiced by the Druze villagers that straddle the Israeli–Syrian border, by the Rastafarians of Jamaica, who identify with Ethiopian beliefs, the Persian followers of Babism, whose adherents gave rise to the Bahá'í faith, the Samaritans, who confine their belief system to a version of the Judaic Torah, the mainly Shia-like Shabbakists of Iraq, and even the insular Yazidis of Syria. The Sabians, who practice a gnostic form of Christianity and revile prophets such as Abraham, admit that their belief system has its roots in Abraham's vision of one God.

Throughout its seventy-plus years of modern history, Israel has been greatly aided by population growth. Israel's annual population growth is two to three percent, which is the highest rate in the West, compared to one percent in the US and an actual negative rate in Europe. Growing antisemitism in Europe, amplified by hostile international organizations, fuels increasing emigration from Europe to Israel.

In the face of rising economic, cultural, and physical pressures from an increasingly irrational and self-destructive Europe and US, Israel must defend its existence and oppose the establishment of a Palestinian state. Maintaining one hundred percent control over Jerusalem, Judea, and Samaria—all of which historically and rightfully belong to Israel—is crucial to the survival of the Jewish State and the well-being of its Jewish, Muslim, and Christian citizens. At the same time, to the extent it can, Israel must maintain the status quo until a more suitable and internationally-supported alternative emerges.

If the PA survives the coming international political upheavals, it—or its recognized replacement—must substantially reinvent its governance and reshape its society. Importantly, the international community, which created the PA during the Oslo process, may soon admit that the interim quasi-governmental entity it created decades ago is long past its usefulness. The PA now stands as the greatest obstacle to peaceful progress.

The PA's devotion to paying terrorists' salaries, its obsession with indoctrinating its citizens, especially its formative youth, with hatred of Jews, and its refusal to enter serious negotiations with Israel disqualify it from further existence unless it can reform and redefine its entire *modus operandi*. Likely, it cannot. Therefore, the task of securing a viable future would fall to the PA's replacement. Replacement leaders have long been waiting in the wings; we see them biding their time in Gulf state capitals. When the replacement leaders are installed, they will reeducate their population and construct the underpinnings of coexistence with Israel, thus enabling prosperity for all—Israelis and Palestinians.

Until a Palestinian governing entity can join the munity of peace-loving nations, no territorial compromises should be considered. No progress with the PA will be possible until all worldwide terror organizations associated with political Islam are defeated, surrender, or reform to join the peaceful civilized world. Such a notion is hardly unrealistic. Egypt, Jordan, the United Arab Emirates, Bahrain, and Morocco are trying to go down the path of peace, and Saudi Arabia appears to be doing the same.

Nonetheless, Arab and Islamic opposition to rational efforts to foster peaceful relations between Israel and its neighbors is formidable. The Organization of Islamic Cooperation (OIC), consisting of 56 countries, the Arab League consisting of 22 countries, and the PA all work to protract the no-war, no-peace status quo. The OIC still seeks world domination, but all must accept the right of Israel to exist as the nation-state of the Jewish people, and the rights of Christians and Hindus to control their own destinies in their home countries. Meanwhile, the PA has perfected its own homegrown false narratives and imaginary history during the past fifty-five years to attempt to deny 3,800 years of Jewish legacy.

The UAE recently created the first crack in the OIC's intransigent bloc by pursuing an historic peace treaty with Israel. The UAE's full, warm, enthusiastic, and strictly bilateral peace agreement, known as the Abraham Accords, proved that forward thinking in the Arab world can unshackle its people from the past and allow them to race toward the future. For example, in July 2020, just prior to gathering the strength to make peace with Israel, the oil-rich UAE switched on its first civilian nuclear reactor.

Quite simply, the UAE–Israeli treaty has neutralized the PA's ability to veto peace. The PA's irrational, hysterical, and anti-factual protestations are now much harder to broadcast—and even harder to swallow.

Yet, standing atop a platform of historical fallacies, the PA still declares its intention to negate the indigenous rights of the Jews. The PA cleverly pretends to represent the rights of the indigenous Palestinian people, so-called refugees, even though the vast majority migrated from Lebanon, Syria, Jordan, and Egypt only in the past 100 years to what would in 1948 become the modern state of Israel. Arab migrants streamed in, searching for work in the newly reestablished Jewish villages and towns that emerged in the twentieth century. The Arab migration process followed basic economics: people go where the jobs are. Although the term now in vogue is "Palestinians," until 1964, when the Palestinian Liberation Organization was invented by the KGB and the Arab League, the universal term for that community in British Palestine was "Arabs." The term Arab was used locally and externally for self-identification and global recognition. Arab was their endonym and exonym.

For generations, Palestinians were Jews dwelling in or resettling in their ancient land: Judea. History knows that after the Jewish expulsion, the Romans erased

Judea (Land of the Jews) from their maps and replaced it with Syria Palaestina—"Syria of the Philistines," which in turn became Palestine. The Romans were accustomed to erasing the names of those they vanquished. Centuries later, when the Ottomans occupied the area, they kept the Romanized name. Regardless of external names tacked onto ancient Jewish lands, the land remained Jewish—whether sovereign or occupied.

The UN has been complicit in the perpetuation of the PA's false narrative. Witness the UN's numerous one-sided resolutions through UNRWA (United Nations Relief and Works Agency) and its mis-education programs, generally run by Hamas on behalf of the Muslim Brotherhood. No wonder that this population cannot break out of its turbulent, leaderless past to grasp the gold ring of peace.

Like the United States, Israel is fighting its own multifront war. The difference: Israel knows it.

The vibrancy and incessantly interactive dynamics of Israel's multifront war carry profound implications for both Israel and the United States should the vaunted two-state solution be implemented. Despite its fleeting appeal, such a development would simultaneously explode into a guaranteed political-military suicide for Israel and America, and a guaranteed economic disaster for Arabs in eastern Jerusalem.

Analyze it. True, a two-state solution is a noble, remote goal that has benefitted from great advertising. But any current move toward a two-state solution is guaranteed to be a failure because the PA has never accepted a two-state solution without the "right of return," which would instantly result in the demise of Israel and slide into a one-state solution.

Guaranteed political-military suicide for Israel means Israel would be forced to give up security control over the West Bank. Hamas (the nearest arm of Iran) would quickly fill the void, thereby surrounding Israel with terror forces and rockets.

Guaranteed political failure for the US means that the Roadmap for Peace in the Middle East process would be guaranteed to fail as well, because the PA and key neighboring states, such as Syria and Iran, have never accepted a two-state solution. Any sudden apparent support for such a plan would be reshaped as fast and unpredictably as all sand-shifting politics in the Mideast. In recent years, Israel's "friendliest" neighbor—Egypt, has reinvented itself several times. This began with peace-evolved-but-assassinated president Anwar Sadat, who was succeeded by authoritarian-but-toppled Hosni Mubarak, followed by a junta led by General Mohamed Hussein Tantawi, which was succeeded by disputed election-victor Mohamed Morsi of the subversive Muslim Brotherhood, who was, in turn, removed in yet another coup, this one led by Abdel Fattah el-Sisi, another military man of moderate thought, who was subsequently elected to the presidency. This type of neck-wrenching political upheaval within a single generation does not justify even momentary confidence.

Guaranteed political demise for Fatah is assured by the two-state solution because the group—like many of its ilk in the Mideast—is an entrenched kleptocracy that enjoys little popular support. Fatah can and will be toppled whenever Hamas, with help from Iran, decides to do so. This was already done in Gaza and would be done again should Hamas be enabled in a unified state.

Economic disaster for Arabs in eastern Jerusalem is unavoidable because that population will immediately lose their Israeli-provided social security and health benefits. Moreover, it is unethical to force these Israeli residents to live under the PA's rule of terror and systematic theft from its own population.

Perhaps the best possible outcome for all is a continuation of the unhappy status quo: autonomy for the Palestinian Arabs (as it now exists in limbo), with Judea and Samaria security remaining in Israeli hands, but with, one hopes, much-improved economic relations between the two parties.

Consequently, the US should focus on fostering economic cooperation between Israelis and the Palestinian Arabs without the formation of a formal state. Statehood in a sea of failed Arab states only assures the desperation that so unavoidably breeds terrorists. A quest for the loftier long-term goal can be reinstated when the political climate allows such thoughts to blossom. Until that better but far-off season, Jerusalem must remain united under Israeli control. The reasons are manifold.

Jerusalem has been the capital city of the Jewish people and no other people for 3,000 years, of both ancient Israel and modern Israel. Arab and Muslim caliphates have functioned in Medina, Damascus, Baghdad, and Cairo—but never in Jerusalem. Jews lived in Jerusalem for 1,700 years before the Arab conquests in the seventh century, and many centuries before the advent of either Christianity or Islam. Scholars often remind us that Jerusalem is mentioned 641 times in the Bible and zero times in the Quran. Jewish legal rights to Jerusalem (and even all of Judea and Samaria) were "irrevocably" recognized in the San Remo Conference of 1920 by unanimous agreement of the 51 members of the League of Nations, which also included approval by Faisal, the Arab leader democratically elected on behalf of the pan-Arab tribes. Moreover, for the past 150 years, the Jewish population in Jerusalem has constituted either a majority or a plurality.

Jews were ethnically cleansed from eastern Jerusalem when they were attacked by five Arab armies and other allied nationals in 1948. This was the second twentieth-century ethnic cleansing of Jews from their homeland by Muslims; the first was committed by the Turks, who expelled tens of thousands of Jews from Tel Aviv and Jaffa during WWI. Remember: in 1949, twenty-five percent of Jerusalem's Jews fled when exposed to random sniper fire from the Arab Legion. Without the Israeli security control that exists today, Jerusalem would again descend into chaos, with rival militias battling each other as they now do in the Gaza Strip. This would make life intolerable to residents, pilgrims, and tourists alike, all of whom are currently assured access to their holy sites in Israel.

Israeli Arab residents in eastern Jerusalem enjoy social security and health insurance benefits valued at about $10,000 per annum. Removing such benefits and ceding this population to a tyrannical regime—whether the nameplate brandishes the logo of the PA, Hamas, or a new hybrid—is both unethical and immoral. It also violates the wishes of the majority of

Arabs in eastern Jerusalem. Arabs in Jerusalem crave stability and access to services.

If Israel were to irrationally allow the establishment of a Palestinian Arab state, the PA would not protect the Christian population or religious sites, as witnessed by the PA's persecution of Christian Arabs in Bethlehem. Nor would Jewish sites be protected, as seen daily and sometimes hourly at Joseph's tomb in Nablus (Shechem), the synagogue in Jericho, or the all-important Tomb of the Patriarchs in Hebron. Between 1948 and 1967, fifty-nine Jewish religious sites were destroyed by the occupying Jordanians.

It gets worse. PA control over eastern Jerusalem would create a magnet for Sunni terror organizations (such as the Muslim Brotherhood, al-Qaeda, the Palestinian Islamic Jihad, as well as Shiite-based terror organizations such as Hezbollah and Hamas). Such a magnet would create an increasingly more powerful threat until it just takes over—as occurred in Lebanon, Gaza, and now, Egypt. In fact, Jerusalem would become a focus of rivalry among these worldwide terror organizations. Hamas is again a formal partner of Fatah in the PA. Hamas has hosted al-Qaeda groups in Gaza since 2006. These increasing hostilities would inevitably guarantee yet another war, which would lead to more rapidly festering tensions worldwide between Jews, Muslims, and Christians.

Beyond forestalling the geopolitical and strategic threats, unified Israeli control of Jerusalem is equally crucial for the Israel Defense Forces (IDF). The city secures the route needed during wartime to move soldiers and equipment to the eastern border along the Jordan River.

Just beyond Jerusalem, we see Judea and Samaria, the two territories Israel must also retain control over. In 1948, these two ancient provinces were nicknamed "the West Bank" after Jordan illegally invaded and occupied the lands. Yet, they have always remained rooted in Jewish identification and legacy. According to the Bible, these two lands were given to the Jews via Abraham some 38 centuries ago. But beyond the biblical text, history and present-day fact unalterably shows that these realms all have historically Jewish names. The very term "Jewish" derives from Judea, the southern kingdom of Israel. Samaria, or Shomron, which means "watchtower" in Hebrew, was named for the capital of the northern kingdom of Israel. The Bible records that Israelite King Omri purchased the land from the man known as Shemer. Shemer was named for Shem, Noah's son, whose descendants gave rise to the "Shemites," the ethnic name that evolved into "Semites."

On the other hand, Arabs—who only in 1964 began calling themselves "Palestinians"—are largely newcomers. The Arabs have always eschewed modernity. The Jews have always embraced modernity.

What's in a name? All Gazans with the common last name of "al-Masri" trace their immediate lineage back to Egypt; al-Masri means "of Egypt." On March 23, 2012, even the Hamas Minister of the Interior and National Security, Fathi Hamad, verified this. He said, "Who are the Palestinians? We have many families called al-Masri, whose roots are Egyptian! They may be from Alexandria, from Cairo, from Damietta, from the north, from Aswan, from Upper Egypt. We are

Egyptians; we are Arabs. We are Muslims. We are part of you. Egyptians! Personally, half my family is Egyptian—and the other half are Saudis." The term "Arab" connotes a descent from the Arabian Peninsula.

Continuing to examine the place names burned into history—Jerusalem, Shiloh, Beit El, Hebron, Kiryat Arba, Efrat, Shechem and some forty other towns, all were mentioned in the Five Books of Moses. None were mentioned in the Quran. The name Hebron derives from the Hebrew word "hevra," that is loosely connoting a circle of friends or citizens.

Quite simply, Judea and Samaria represent the eastern border of Western civilization. Remembering that the name *Samaria* derives from the Hebrew term for watchtower, it is understood that when those twin territories fall, the rest of Israel beyond those lines falls next. When the eastern bulwark of Western civilization—Israel—falls, the final Islamist invasion of Europe follows. With Israel weakened or gone, Iran will be able attack or intimidate the Sunni countries in order to control their oil—and exert control over world oil prices. Iran's Hezbollah agents will then be liberated to expand their narco-terrorism in Latin America and into the US.

With Jewish and Sunni enemies neutralized, Iran will expand its nuclear bomb and long-range missile capability, in turn, intimidating or destroying non-submissive Christians—first in Europe and then in the US. America's 2020 election has weakened America and unhinged its doors. The country has been teetering on the verge of an armed civil war over culture, history, its past failures, and its own precarious future. A weakened political and civil leadership would substantially lessen its resolve. Many in the Middle East already contemplate such a scenario. A nuclear Iran will lead to a nuclear Saudi Arabia, followed by a nuclear Egypt and Turkey, followed by others.

Nuclear proliferation in the region would rapidly increase the chances of an eventual nuclear war or nuclear terrorism. Recall that the cataclysmic run-up to World War I—the still-inexplicable conflict that killed millions in so many countries—was mainly ignited by the assassination of an archduke in a carriage on a street in Serbia. Think of WWI, with its endlessly shifting alliances, competing armies, scorched earth, and dead multitudes—and now replace the primitive tanks and machine guns of that era with modern missiles and nuclear weapons.

A healthy and secure Israel is in America's security and strategic interest for an array of proven reasons. In a world where Muslims are fiercely pitted against non-Muslims—in the Indian sub-continent, North America, Latin America, Europe and even the Philippines—Israel remains the only country where Jews, Christians and Muslims coexist peacefully. This fact is proven daily despite ceaseless and sensationalized headlines and professional agitators. Tens of thousands of Arabs from the West Bank line up daily for lucrative equal employment in Israel. The Jewish State's citizenry is 20 percent Arab, and that community wields a pivotal 15 percent legislative bloc. In a region that abhors religious minorities and historically has proved its willingness to kill them mercilessly, only Israel guarantees complete freedom of religion.

Israeli ingenuity pumps a steady stream of medical, scientific, and military innovation into America—from cell phone technology to computer chips, to the hundreds of start-ups that gave the Jewish nation its hip moniker "start-up nation." Go no further than the traffic-mapping cell phone app Waze, the chatting app WhatsApp, America's drone fleet, and the explosive protective armor on Army tanks to see a fraction of what Israel provides to the American way of life. Intelligence and cyber research stand apart as a special gleaming sphere of US cooperation with Israel because a plethora of Israeli intel obliges Israel to interface minute-to-minute with their American counterparts. Joint projects in the works include missile defense shields of inestimable value. Two-thirds of the foreign aid we provide annually to Israel returns to the US, contributing to the vibrant American workforce and the resilient American economy. Israel has become a precious fountain of innovation which must be preserved for good.

Without Israel, America would find it impossible to perceive, confront, and do battle in its multifront war.

Chapter Five: America's Willful Blindness

America is facing multiple threats to its existence but does not recognize it. No fewer than ten fronts occupy the foreground, but the country does not see them as interconnected menaces. These fronts span the threat spectrum from missiles to money laundering to multinational NGOs.

First, Iranian ICBMs and EMP weapons, while not yet fully operational, are nonetheless important enough to the Kremlin to be protected by Russian air defenses. Moscow's S-300 state-of-the-art air defense system has built a formidable shield—and is even now being rapidly replaced by the S-400, making it even more difficult to neutralize Iran's offensive weapons.

Second, the fuzzy conglomerate of international and multinational organizations, such as the European Union and the United Nations, allied with NGOs, has worked intensely to delegitimize the defenses and credibility of both America and its allies.

Third, the chronic underfunding of NATO means the defense pact is overshadowed by Russian "active measures" and political Islam, neither of which is in NATO's current purview.

Fourth, while weaknesses and self-imposed paralysis limit our responses, Iran continues its quiet invasion of Latin America and Africa.

Fifth, external threats are matched by corresponding internal threats, as Marxism, socialism, and antisemitism accelerate, transplanting these poisonous ideologies to US shores and reinfecting much of the country, especially our universities, the mass media, and Hollywood.

Sixth, we are weakened even further by the actions of the Islamist movement, not only within our governmental apparatus but also by that organization's robust prison radicalization program and its push to enable Sharia supremacy over our legal system.

Seventh, we see Iran and ISIS on our southern border, manifested through drug trafficking organizations and transnational criminal organizations.

Eighth, from Asia, the North Korean threat looms as the rogue regime approaches the point of no return, when their long-range nuclear-tipped missiles can survive reentry into the upper atmosphere. North Korea is just an appendage of the larger China threat, which is expanding its scheme to steal our intellectual property wholesale. What's more, it pursues economic hegemony through its Belt and Road Initiative, formerly known as One Belt One Road. China's goal is to ensure "Made in China" dominance by 2025.

Ninth, cyber warfare, hovers over all other threats.

The tenth threat is growing mis-education in our colleges and universities.

Moreover, America is losing ground on virtually all ten of these national security fronts. Why? Because the country's leaders have ignored their responsibility to develop a comprehensive multifront strategy to defend the nation. Numbness can only be achieved by willful blindness, exacerbated by the acceptance of foreign financial contributions and foreign business opportunities. A graphic example is Boeing's outreach to Iran to consummate a multibillion-dollar commercial aircraft order. Such a deal would obviously generate welcomed jobs in the US, but would simultaneously facilitate Iran's movement of weapons and terrorists throughout the world. Iran will not make polite distinctions between commercial and military uses of aviation. Fortunately, the Trump administration killed this particular deal, but this is just a fraction of the threat fast approaching through commercial vectors.

Latent antisemitism often clouds the ability of our leaders to protect US national security. Many leaders are loath to get involved in the plight of Jews in general and Israel, in particular. They do not seem to realize that the fates of Jews and Christians are tied together. Jews are simply the canaries in the coal mine.

Problems and challenges that originate in Israel and the greater Middle East will soon proliferate into Europe and the US. This is beginning in front of our eyes right now. Our political leaders have yet to internalize that public criticisms of antisemitism and racism should, in general, be made on a nonstop basis and at all levels of government. Anti-racism laws must be enforced on behalf of all victims of bigotry, whatever their color, race, or creed. President Trump's recent executive order extending Title VI protections to Jewish students is a big step in the right direction. Two Title VI provisions exist—one arising from the 1964 Civil Rights Act and the second from various streams of education legislation, such as the Education Amendments of 1972. Both extend hate speech protections to Jews, even for their identity as Zionists based on religion. The Title VI executive order must be raised as a shield and paired with an enforcement sword. Until then, it is just more willful blindness.

What's more, the US must combat both physical and cultural terror threats. Presently, it faces physical Islamist terror entities financed by the supporters of Islamism, such as Iran, ISIS, al-Qaeda, and the Muslim Brotherhood. The key challenge is to bring into focus that cultural terrorism and physical terrorism are interrelated. If cultural terrorism is allowed to infiltrate schools, books, the nation's mosques, America's prison system, and social media for the first twenty years of someone's life, the transformation to physical terrorism will become the logical next step when an individual comes of age. This reality has played out daily in recent months as we see anarchic, socialistic, and chaotic mob rule singe and burn many of our cities.

The radical leftist and Islamist enemies of the US appear to be working together in some cases. Both are unabashedly consumed by their inherent need to gain political power for power's sake—the hallmark of totalitarianism. Progressive and radical left NGOs, many of which are financed by billionaires and their foundations, represent a political threat to the US. These NGOs undermine American and Western values, while unethically taking advantage of our federal government and public taxpayer subsidies through their tax exemptions.

Ultra-progressive billionaire and megadonor George Soros pumped millions of dollars into massive funding of progressive local prosecutors with radical ideas on criminal justice. For example, in October 2019, Soros foundations spent more than $800,000 on behalf of a progressive newcomer in a local race in Rochester, New York. In St. Louis, $78,700 was donated to the prosecutor who indicted a husband and wife for reacting with pointed firearms to threatening rioters encroaching on their property. These massive outside cash infusions for local elections can dwarf local candidates' campaign resources. A related $220 million was donated by Soros to organizations with an eye toward overhauling our system top to bottom. Within that $220 million is $150 million granted to various civil rights and racial equality groups like Black Voters Matter and the Equal Justice Initiative, groups that wish to completely revamp our justice and criminal codes.

Before our very eyes, cultural domestic terror organizations are now morphing into physical terror organizations, as can be witnessed by the rise of Black Lives Matter (BLM) and Antifa. Black Lives Matter may have begun as a noble thought and an uplifting slogan that blossomed out of the smoldering ash of slavery and twentieth-century Jim Crow and other racist laws. Like many similar movements, it has been hijacked by committed Marxists and anarchists, who easily morph into fascism while pretending to be anti-fascist. This morphing and hijacking of legitimately needed protest and pushback yielded the sudden rise of socialist mainstreaming and the violent, ready-to-rumble Antifa.

Remember, fascist and white supremacist groups exist as outliers in our country—justly termed "fringe groups." It might be argued that they represent a fraction of a single percent of the US population. Yet, the most radical leftist groups are protected by organizations such as the Southern Poverty Law Center

(SPLC) and the American Civil Liberties Union (ACLU), brandishing copies of the Constitution. The SPLC even publishes a list of hate groups and websites, which often includes some that clearly possess pro-American values, while the ACLU protects hate sites run by Islamist cultural and physical terror organizations.

The Red-Green Alliance of leftists and Islamists has become increasingly dangerous as their false narrative ideologies have mutually embraced the most nefarious aspects of each other's propaganda message strategies. The Reds have adopted the Green strategy of *taqiyya*—the Quranic blessing of dissimulation or deception when engaged in combat. The Greens have adopted the Reds' patience in infiltrating schools, universities, courts, and all levels of government. Both have used projection and transference to accuse their opponents of doing what they are actually doing. Each cherishes the ultimate goal of undermining and supplanting our culture until we lose confidence in our way of life. It appears to be working.

For example, the recent understandable effort to remove Civil War statues—the erection of which confounded reason by honoring true enemies of the United States—is just a gateway to acid washing other notable pillars of our history, including George Washington, Abraham Lincoln, Ulysses Grant, and a whole community of abolitionists as part of mass cultural erasure. One could speculate that that would ultimately lead to the argument that the Constitution was written by racists and must therefore be rejected. Actually, that question has already been decided; the *New York Times* spearheaded "The 1619 Project." This project turns our nation away from our traditional Fourth of July observances to a total reframing of

American history as a slavery enterprise that began in 1619. In this new narrative, there is no mention of the indispensable Arab slave trade and its local African collaborators, who made it possible for millions of innocent Africans to be kidnapped and brought into the caliphates of the Muslim world as well as into the Western Hemisphere to live a life of degrading enslavement. It was American exceptionalism and the drive to be free that led us to the unshackling from this dark, centuries-long European–Arab–African legacy within a single American generation. The US announced a ban on the importation of slaves in 1807; the ban went into effect on January 1, 1808. True, one must always tether that accomplishment to the dismal reality that the true light of emancipation was controlled not by a large light switch but by a generations-long slow dimmer dial. Fifteen centuries of slavery could not be erased with mere paper edicts or good intentions. It has been very much a work in progress and is integral to America's democratic system. In the meantime, the Islamist tradition of enslaving Africans and others continues throughout the Arab world to this day. ISIS proved that in Syria when the area came under their control with the immediate reestablishment of slave markets.

As this page is read, millions of modern-day Africans are still enslaved by Arab and Muslim nations. In Mauritania alone, which only technically outlawed slavery in 2007, tens of thousands of African slaves still toil in humiliating bondage. Exactly how many is still debated. In 2013, the Global Slavery Index estimated there were 140,000 slaves in Mauritania, but in 2018, it stated the situation had improved and only 90,000 remained in bondage. In 2017, the BBC reported

600,000 remained captive in that country. Today, Libyan slave markets can deliver a human into a life of forced labor in wealthy Arab countries for a mere $500.

Sanctuary cities—cities or regions that limit cooperation with federal immigration enforcement agents in order to protect certain illegal immigrants from deportation, are spreading throughout America, focusing false narratives into centers of urban upheaval. These cities are becoming more and more lawless and must be curbed. Federal financing must be terminated for sanctuary cities. Some argue that the federal government should actually arrest several key sanctuary-observing and federal law-breaking governors and mayors. That is a long argument better held among jurists and constitutional experts than summarized here in a single paragraph.

While scholars debate, American freedom and democracy must still be protected. To preserve democracy's most quintessential gift, ensuring voter integrity is paramount. Identification laws must prevail in all states. Vote harvesting is fraught with problems and must be disallowed. Inadequate voter protection laws rob all lawful Americans of their electoral right and illegally transfer those rights from lawful politicians and citizens into the hands of illegal immigrants and other non-citizens.

Each day that we ignore these issues, the situation worsens. It will not be possible to say we did not see it coming. It will have been willful blindness in the face of a multifront war.

Chapter Six: The Accelerating Islamization of Europe

It is now clear that European countries are incapable of defending themselves because they do not recognize their own simultaneous multifront national security challenges.

The likely number one threat is Iran's nuclear missile program, which, in many ways, is spawned by the North Korean threat. Iran is developing long-range missiles—not to strike Tel Aviv or the Saudi oil fields, but to reach Brussels, Berlin, and even the British Isles.

Second would be Russia's *aktivnye meropriyatiya*, "active measures," aimed at European nations. This term refers to the ongoing practice of Russian intelligence services to disrupt and impact world events. Their well-honed techniques include faking and transmitting official documents for disinformation or propaganda, provoking political repression, planting fake stories in the media, and even assassination. When Russian or former Soviet bloc intelligence services assassinate someone, they generally do not employ a sniper with a rifle and scope, but rather a faceless member of the crowd carrying an umbrella tipped with a deadly toxin, as was famously done by Bulgarian agents.

Third is political Islam, driven by organizations affiliated with the Muslim Brotherhood—already banned in many Arab countries and labeled a terrorist group by most. Egypt, Saudi Arabia, and the Gulf States are among those who have outlawed this group, but the Brotherhood still has active operations in Europe.

Fourth is an unending wave of illegal, mostly Muslim migration from Europe's flank via the Mediterranean, the Aegean Sea, and the Balkans to Greece, Italy, and Spain. War-ravaged Syria has produced a heartbreaking font of people seeking escape and a better life. While many Syrian migrants are fleeing economic, cultural, and political chaos in their home countries, as a group, they have not acted according to established refugee laws, wherein the first safe terrestrial point of landing becomes their safe haven. In large caravans, they have been unwilling to accept safety and settle in Greece, Italy, Bulgaria, or wherever they first touch the continent. Instead, they demand unimpeded passage to Germany, Scandinavia, and Belgium, where social welfare rules are more liberal.

In 2020, Muslim migrants began crossing the English Channel in small boats to settle in Great Britain. Setting fires, overwhelming walls, and pilfering along the way, they are aided and encouraged by the Turkish government and other vectors of the MB in their advance en masse through the continent. Vociferously, caravan leaders warn that they intend to flaunt local laws, culture, and tradition in favor of establishing Sharia, transplanting their legacy of hate for other religions, and their institutional victimization of women. These highly publicized waves of refugees are not predominantly huddled masses of families yearning to be free, but virile, fighting-age men demanding to set up shop in an affluent country of their choice. Some have filmed themselves gleefully warning that they shall marry the daughters of receiving countries and convert a generation to Islam. These mass migrations are not free to the refugees, who have paid a comparative fortune to human traffickers, thus enriching and enlarging a vile channel of dangerous commerce. In this horror show, rape and enslavement are the international currency of population transfer. In time, this migration may become Europe's number one existential threat.

Fifth, a concomitant mass migration has flowed not from the Middle East but all of Africa—especially North Africa. As we see the agony of destitute masses, once again, we see a from them a desire to not just set foot on any inch of safe soil on Europe's southern coasts, but to become an unstoppable throng determined to pick new homes from among the northern climes. They are victimized once again by the monetary fortune they remit to human traffickers. Africans have been exploited by Arabs for more than a thousand years. Rape and enslavement have become inevitable parts of the transit tariff levied on refugees from African nations as well.

Sixth, European nations suffer from a profusion of Islamic warriors, born and raised in those nations, but indoctrinated in local mosques to reject their new national cultures. Theirs is a culture of alienation, where citizens are *in* a society but not *of* the society. Whether by imposed adverse and subordinated status or their own personal social exit decisions, such people live in a world they despise and have no stake in. Many such people have grown up in Europe's Muslim communities, producing, in essence, a jihadi mill. When given a chance, these fighters have gone to fight for the cause of Islamism with ISIS, brutally murdering both fellow Muslims and fellow countrymen, at home and abroad. When the self-appointed Caliphate fell, these warriors returned to their native lands trained and ready to continue their jihad against perceived enemies at home.

Seventh, Europe remains a target for cyber threats from Iran, China, and Russia. These intruders are more than digital highwaymen and hackers. Iran, China, and Russia are stealing industrial, scientific, and defense secrets, siphoning off generations of modernity and military sinew, until the Sick Man of Europe becomes not just one nation, as it was in the buildup to World War I, but the full membership of the European Union. The Sick Men of Europe are now wobbling in the run-up to a fast-percolating, indistinct international conflict.

As expected, Europe is losing on every front. The key challenge for European countries is that the EU is ruled by 705 multinational legislators sitting in the planet's second largest parliament. While it is true that Members of European Parliament (MEPs) stand for local elections, the EU's Enforcement Commission and its policymaking bureaucracy constitute the true power and decision-making apparatus. The 27–person European Commission sets the true agenda. Through its MEPs, the Commission can impose Balkan votes on Scandinavia, east European decisions on the heart of central Europe and so on, through the far-flung territorial reach of the legislators. But the policies, controls, and priorities originate in the Commission. While the European land mass may very roughly compare to that of the US, in Europe, the culture of Iceland is not the same as that of Sicily. The net result is that the European Commission has tried to create its own horse, and as might be expected, produced a camel. The beast can become so humped that nations rebel for the sake of their heritages—as Brexit has proved.

The consequences of unelected governance apply widely to the EU. Through phalanxes of unaccountable bureaucrats, the European Commission inflicts decrees. The EU uses "hate speech" laws to disguise the reality of the internal threats largely caused by the flood of illegal Muslim refugees. In consequence, Europe is institutionally incapable of solving its key problems on a day-to-day basis. It is not so much that the emperor has no clothes; it is that he lurches beneath so many layers of costume that he is crushed under their weight.

Notably, the European Union began its existence as a price-fixing fuel cartel, the European Coal and Steel Community (ECSC), a fuel market combine not unlike OPEC. The list of products and prices to be fixed was expanded to create the overarching Common Market, which functioned under various phased reorganizations and names, but most recognizable as the European Economic Community (EEC).

The Islamization of Europe began in earnest with the return to power of General Charles de Gaulle in 1958 and the subsequent loss of the Algerian war in 1962. Having lost the various colonies in North Africa it had accumulated during the previous 125 years, France decided to try to unite these former colonies into an economic sphere with Europe, largely managed by France and Germany. This policy additionally distanced Europe from the US, which had saved Europe twenty years earlier during WWII. Europe further distanced itself from the US and moved closer to the Muslim world in 1967, in the face of an OPEC oil embargo following Israel's victory in the Six Day War. Europe quickly became subservient to the Muslim world, which never hid its contempt for what it has often jeered as a "continent of *dhimmis*." (*Dhimmitude* is the second-class citizenship status accorded to Jews and Christians under Islamic law.)

Brexit, the UK's popular referendum to withdraw from the EU, was a great victory for Western civilization and a great defeat for the forces of globalism throughout the EU. Globalism is a creature spawned by unelected governance. With Brexit in 2020, the UK reclaimed its sovereignty; and Britain, theoretically, regained control over its own borders and culture. Without these controls, it would be further invaded until its cultural death, as is happening in continental Europe.

Brexit is now a huge test for the UK and will be for years. Great Britain must continue on the path to regain its independence and sovereignty while maintaining its economic strength through renegotiating trade deals with Europe, the US, and other major countries. Meanwhile, the EU will seek to blackmail the UK to the maximum extent possible. When push comes to shove, the UK may well have to accept the aftermath of a hard Brexit to detach itself from a dying EU. Remember, the

EU's emperor is not embarrassed by lack of clothing; rather, so many heavy overlapping garments make his movements disjointed and dangerous.

Ensuing elections and coalition governments in the third decade of the twenty-first century, notably in Germany and the Netherlands, will further challenge the self-destruction embraced by the key governments of Europe. Euroskeptic parties are expected to gain strength and perhaps even topple one or two of the drifted-away governments, as happened in Italy in 2018. In time, these Euroskeptic parties may well topple virtually all the current ruling parties. The challenge will be to keep them democratic and prevent them from swinging the other way toward authoritarianism.

Business influences can wield a deleterious effect on rational foreign policy, especially when the business is conducted with terror states. Increasing business relations directly and indirectly strengthens such terror states. Each such commercial deal undermines Western values even as it swells the pocketbook. Europe's willingness to negotiate business deals with Iran, the number one terror organization in the world, is a graphic case in point. Such conflicts of interest most likely encouraged European leaders to agree to the worst international deal ever agreed to by Western leaders since the Munich Accord with Hitler in 1938. The Iran nuclear deal was seemingly driven by nuclear policy—but everyone knows that purchases of jet planes from Airbus and Boeing created the lift to make the deal airborne.

Further stress arises from the demographic shift gripping the continent. The suffocating dominance of political correctness, slow-growing economies, rising socialism, an inadequate military, and handcuffed law enforcement weakens the fabric of the culture within European nations even as Muslim populations rise to 25–45 percent in most countries. It is key to remember that the Islamic religion is not under scrutiny here in any way—only the considerable fraction of it that manifests jihadism, political Islam, and separatism. Part and parcel of this trend is the new factor of dhimmitude in many European countries. Only those in Eastern Europe have strenuously resisted it. Why? After suffering under Soviet-imposed state socialism during 1946–1989, Eastern European citizens possess a strong skepticism about government propaganda and social programs, particularly surrounding poorly conceived immigration and economic policies.

Hungary, the Czech Republic, Poland, and Slovakia in 1991 formed the Visegrád Group (V4), a cultural and political alliance. The V4 seem to be heading in the right direction. All are members of the EU and NATO, but are refusing to accept the European Commission's immigration quotas, rightly arguing that the waves of mostly Muslim migrants are creating parallel societies that, in turn, undermine their nations' cultural integrity, economic, political and national security, and endanger public health. The V4 and other European nations who have objected the EC's imposed immigration quotas have been censured, dragged to the European Court, and are under constant attack by left-leaning local and international media (*NYT,* CNN, and the BBC, to name a few), plus well-funded international NGOs, and the UN.

For example, Hungary's Prime Minister Viktor Orbán has been widely attacked for his resistance to immigration quotas. On July 26, 2016, he said, "Hungary does not need a single migrant for the economy to work, or the population to sustain itself, or for the country to have a future. Every single migrant poses a public security and terror risk. This is why there is no need for a common European migration policy: whoever needs migrants can take them, but don't force them on us; we don't need them." Orbán continued, "For us, migration is not a solution but a problem... not medicine but a poison. We don't need it and won't swallow it." Orbán has been almost universally condemned for this and other statements decrying efforts to force Hungary to accept an arbitrary number of Muslim and African migrants.

Hopefully, the members of V4 group will both remain strong and encourage the EU's other Member States to refuse the EC's dictates on migrant quotas.

Rough urban neighborhoods are as old as cities. They come in all complexions and socio-economic makeups and can be found throughout America and the world. Many become dangerous to outsiders after sunset. But the proliferation of ethnically contentious zones in countries such as Sweden, Belgium, France, Denmark, Germany, and even the UK has added a new dimension. Such zones can lead to demands for autonomy—from Seattle's CHOP to Free Derry in

Northern Ireland to hundreds of neighborhoods declared by France to be *Zones Urbaines Sensibles*. Ethnically contentious zones can lead to calls for autonomy which can eventually lead to calls for separatism. Separatism fosters the drive to create separate states and may ignite civil wars. Many experts predict that within ten to twenty years, virtually all democratic European countries will have no choice but to declare martial law (as France did for six months in 2015) to protect their populations from political Islam, and to avoid civil wars bursting forth in virtually every western European country.

Both globalism and statism pose major risks to the proper functioning of any democratic nation-state. Individual European countries must reclaim their sovereignty and control over their borders. The EU must be reconfigured into a free trade association and must stop mismanaging the security affairs of Europe as a whole, as well as those of individual countries. European countries must relearn what has lately been called "the virtue of nationalism," based on common values and shared legacies, meaning a return to classic self-determination as envisioned after WWI. The EU governmental superstructure and bureaucracy has proven itself incapable of protecting Europe from both cultural and physical terror organizations. It has, thereby, forgone its right to rule in its current configuration with its current leadership. It must be dismantled for the good of its members and their citizens.

Population trends in Europe must be reversed to restore the status quo ante. With indigenous Europeans producing only about 1.5 babies per family versus 3 to 5 babies for recently arrived Muslim families, many western European countries are projected to become Muslim-majority countries between 2050 and 2100.

Unfortunately, democracies generally only make important decisions during times of huge stress—internal or external. Democracy is a very reactive form of government. Problems and challenges inevitably fester until an escalating crisis provokes a response.

Multiplying crises are guaranteed to arise until new European governments take power with the mandate to protect their citizens. That cannot occur until the entire continent corrects its visual acuity and properly perceives the constellation of crises mounting from without and within as part of a multifront war.

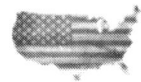

Chapter Seven: Stopping Iran

The terrorist state of Iran is the greatest threat to the US, to Israel, to Sunni Muslim countries, and to Europe. As part of the Joint Comprehensive Plan of Action (JCPOA), commonly referred to as the Iran Nuclear Deal, Iran was gifted a $150 billion windfall. Much of the money was delivered in cash in the middle of the night by the Obama administration. This unprecedented signing bonus is a direct result of poor negotiating strategy by some and purposeful negligence by others among the P5+1 (US, Great Britain, France, Russia, and China plus Germany) nations. An additional $1.8 billion in cash was given by the US as ransom payments for hostages. No one knows where this cash went, but direct payments to terror organizations and to the leaders of various Western countries is a good guess. Then-Secretary of State John Kerry refused to dispute that probability in public statements. In fact, the Obama administration at numerous levels consistently acknowledged that these funds might well further expand Iran's terror network throughout the Middle East, Africa, and Latin America, and would indisputably aid Iran's business, political, and cultural influence throughout the world.

Iran continues to gain strength precisely because the major world powers are unwilling to stop it. The parallels to WWII are deeply troubling. Think back: when the UK, France, and Russia refused to stop the

German rearmament in the 1930s, this paved the way to full-scale war in the 1940s, with sixty million consequential but largely unnecessary deaths. Those sixty million deaths, coming only 25 years after the deaths of thirty million Europeans in WWI, piled atop the approximately 2.5 million casualties of the 1917–18 influenza pandemic, sapped Europe's willingness to defend itself.

Iran is not only challenging the West for regional and world dominance; it is also challenging the Sunnis' dominance in the Islamic world. Sunnis account for some 85 percent of Muslims worldwide. Tehran is the epicenter of apocalyptic Shia Islam, which is practiced by only 15 percent of the world's Muslims. These dwell mainly in Iran and parts of southern Iraq, with the rest scattered among other nations. Many Shias revile Sunnis, and many Sunnis revile Shiites. This revulsion and inter-denominational conflagration have defined the two groups since Islam's schism in 632 CE, which arose from the dispute over who would succeed Muhammad following his death.

During the twenty-first century, Iran has executed a well-formulated strategy to take over Iraq, Syria, Lebanon, and Yemen, and then penetrate further into Africa. In this quest, the mullahs of Tehran are aided by branches of Al-Mustafa University in seventeen countries, as well as more than eighty cultural centers in several Latin American nations. Among its Latin American penetrations, Iran's growing base in Venezuela is one of the deepest.

Within the coming few years, Iran, and, by extension, its partner North Korea, will acquire the capability to effectively attack US and European electrical infrastructure. Sharing intercontinental ballistic missile (ICBM) and nuclear technology, as well as biological warfare research, Iran and North Korea are moving closer to having the ability to place a handful of nuclear weapons into the atmosphere above American or European cities. Two or three such weapons with specialized electromagnetic pulse (EMP) capabilities could destroy our electrical grid for years to come. Iran and North Korea are rapidly improving their cyberwarfare capabilities as well as their supersonic missiles. Cyberwarfare offers an additional method of destroying our electrical grids. Iran and North Korea are positioning themselves to destroy our modernity and very way of life. These capabilities could be used to blackmail the US financially and politically and could also neutralize our cyberwarfare defenses and nuclear capabilities. Additional potential avenues of attack include "dirty bombs"—radioactivity dispersion devices that can contaminate large areas, and well-placed biological agents. Iran and North Korea, shoulder-to-shoulder, are building formidable parallel arsenals.

It comes as no surprise that both Iran and North Korea are sick societies. The word *sick* is used advisedly.

Iran kills its gays in grotesque public hangings, often sadistically swinging victims from construction cranes. The regime subjugates women, while "temporary marriages" of a day or two—prostitution by any other name—are rampant. Sexually transmitted diseases (STDs) afflict more than half the population, according to a sheaf of international academic and medical studies. This has caused Iran's birth rate to plummet from 6.93 children per family in 1960 to 2.12 per family in 2017. Add to that Iran's fractured health care system, and it is no wonder that STDs have become a leading cause of debilitation and death in Iran.

North Korea is not outdone in its societal psychopathy. The regime has locked up an estimated quarter-million of its citizens in hellish re-education camps and prisons without basic necessities or rights. The phrase "without basic necessities or rights" is inadequate. One report told of frail old women compelled to work in massive cow dung vats to gather handfuls of manure for agricultural fertilizer. One reportedly faltered, fell beneath the surface, and slowly perished. Other reports speak of children struggling to retrieve undigested corn kernels from cow manure. Pregnant women are forced to have abortions or to have delivery induced prematurely—and then weep in utter despair as they watch specially trained "nurses" commit monstrous, gruesome infanticide.

Both regimes are at risk for popular uprisings, potentially leading to regime change. Due to Western government incompetence and indifference, the 2009 unrest in 25 Iranian cities was not seized upon as a golden opportunity to assist in such a regime change. The Trump administration has been more active in supporting the new protest movements of 2019–2020. These protests sprang from a normal, popular desire for basic freedoms, intensified by the economic discontent caused by increased US and international trade sanctions. Since increased sanctions have been implemented, Iran has suffered an annual ten percent contraction in GDP, which in the fourth quarter of 2020 almost tripled to an economy-shattering 27 percent.

Iran is far more prepared for WWIII than America and the rest of the West, as delineated in its Constitution, in which Chapter 4 and Articles 43–52 set forth an economy defined as a spiritual and religious achievement, with wealth and enjoyment being secondary, if not tertiary. Chapter 13 establishes a National Security Council under strict theocratic control. Hence, for Iran's leaders, every war is a religious war, where the Quran, Sharia, and jihad serve as military doctrine. Iranian fighters in the Iran–Iraq War of the 1980s were even dispatched to the front lines carrying their own coffins. During that war, some ten thousand children were deliberately sent racing across fields of land mines to clear the path for troops. Each child was holding a symbolic key to heaven. A half-million toy keys had been imported from Taiwan for the purpose. That ghoulish tactic of mass child sacrifice still lives in Iran's military mind, evidenced by a 2019 boast by Mohammad Bathaei, former Minister of Education, who said, "Now, we have 14 million students in schools ... who, if needed, are ready to sacrifice their lives, like the prior period of holy defense in the Iran–Iraq War."

Mutually assured destruction, the precept that has arguably averted an all-out hot war among the nuclear powers, will not deter the ayatollahs. Tehran's theocratic leaders will relish the spilled blood if the outcome fits their apocalyptic vision of heaven and earth. Iran's youthful population wants to live and thrive, but the killing buttons and commands of war are under the control of the mullahs, who can decide for a million of their own—and for a million of our own. America is seen less as an enemy and more of a religious scourge to be annihilated—the "Great Satan."

Iran is fully prepared for WWIII. As of now, no Western country is organized to manage or protect itself in a comparable manner. As it girds itself, Iran's leaders believe it is leading an effort to take over the world as part of a holy Islamic revolution commanded by Allah.

Despite Iran's conduct in plain sight, aided by increasingly aggressive financial backing from China, we in the West have refused to acknowledge that we are already in the opening volleys of WWIII and, by that refusal, we are losing on all fronts. We are now organizationally unprepared to fight—and win—WWIII. Iran is.

Iran is already waging a multifront war. We are not.

Chapter Eight: China Ascending, Russia Resurging

While we face numerous enemies, our two major adversaries are also our two major competitors: China and Russia. The Chinese and the Russians have already succeeded in filling the void created by President Obama's deliberate withdrawal from world affairs. Russia continues to expand its presence in Crimea, Ukraine, Syria, Lebanon, Iraq, Iran, and Latin America. China continues to surge throughout the South China Sea, the Indian Ocean as well as in Southeast Asia, Central Asia, Africa, Latin America, and the extended Middle East, especially Iran and Turkey.

China's key advantage is its huge size and strength relative to its far smaller neighbors. Its foreign policy is bold, exemplified by its establishment of a massive naval presence in the South and East China Seas and its creation of what are essentially artificial islands, built up in disputed territory. For example, Woody Island covered just about one square mile until China claimed it and installed strategic harbors deep enough to receive its aircraft carriers. China also built a 2,700-meter military runway, long enough to accommodate Beijing's most advanced fighter jets, and a causeway to another tiny island. These constitute a string of far forward military bases.

China is also rebuilding the ancient Silk Road through its Belt and Road initiative—an unprecedented infrastructure project. At a cost of approximately $1 trillion, the physical portion of the road will course through some seventy countries, connecting continents via thousands of miles of roadway. The Belt and Road project is the twenty-first century version of the Han Dynasty's legendary trade route system, which from 206 BCE to 220 CE forged China's merchant networks throughout Central Asia and the Asian subcontinent. The asphalt road is complemented by a Maritime Silk Road and a Digital Silk Road. These developments will certainly boost economic growth in every region they touch, from Asia to Europe and Africa. In the process, Chinese economic and political influence will soar. Many of these linked local projects are based on well-calculated loans from China. Local governments will eventually default on much of this debt, thereby allowing China to seize key infrastructure projects, many of which have dual economic and military use. In anticipation of such outcomes, Chinese enterprises are already investing heavily throughout the world, particularly in Asia, Africa, and Latin America.

The "Made in China 2025" program is another massive initiative to upgrade Chinese industry. Its key focus is to increase the domestic component of core materials from 35 percent in 2018 to 70 percent by 2025. If successful, China will become the world leader, dominating ten major high technology markets:

- information technology
- aerospace equipment
- ocean engineering
- railway equipment
- power equipment
- new materials

- medicines
- medical devices
- agricultural machinery
- green energy

In the process, China would come to dominate in artificial intelligence and the Internet of Things (IoT), wielding a commanding control of connected smart devices from smart appliances in the home to smart cities across the nation. What's more, China would rule the realms of energy efficiency, electric vehicles, and next-generation maritime vessels. Communist China would not only out-produce the world—it would control that production, essentially locking us into a tech cold war.

Beijing's scheme to control everything is advancing by leaps and bounds precisely because China excels in stealing Western technology and intellectual property. The Chinese are also adept at cyberwarfare. Notably, the civilian and military needs of the country are integrated through its civil–military fusion doctrine.

China excels at intimidating those in its geographic sphere, such as Taiwan and Hong Kong, Japan, South Korea, and Vietnam. Not bound by geography, China exerts educational pressure on distant countries through hundreds of its Confucius Institutes. Many of these ostensible language and cultural centers now exist at major US schools and universities, where they connect with Chinese students, prepare the general student body for Chinese interaction and intimidate the entertainment and media industries. As of 2019, there were more than 500 Confucius Institutes in countries on six continents. China's Ministry of Education aims to double the number every few years. In the US, however, campus and governmental opposition have frustrated or ejected many of these Institutes. In 2019, federal legislation barred them from American universities that receive Pentagon funding. As a result of this legislation, many universities have shuttered their Confucius Institutes. These include Indiana University, the University of Minnesota, the University of Oregon, University of Rhode Island, San Francisco State University, Arizona State University, and San Diego State University. More colleges and universities will follow suit now that an August 2020 Department of State decision has designated Confucius Institutes as "foreign missions" of the People's Republic of China.

Other nations are beginning to take similar action. For example, in 2020, Sweden ended all Confucius Institute programming in its country. However, doing so risks trade retaliation, so only the stronger nations have started closing their centers. Still, Beijing can and will easily rename the Institutes and embed them throughout the world. China is already deeply invested in higher education.

Since the start of this century, the Chinese Communist Party has dramatically expanded its involvement with universities, both within its borders and abroad. Chinese college graduates now constitute nearly 10 million persons, or approximately 20 percent of all college students worldwide. This rising brain trust has led to the proliferation of new innovative companies, the biggest and best of which have had over 175 initial public offerings (IPOs) in both Hong Kong and the US in the second decade of this century.

Competing with China for supremacy and control is Russia. The Russian bear is back; the wounds from its Soviet-era decline are no longer visible. Moscow's key advantage is its huge oil and natural gas production and reserves, which China lacks. Unlike other oil and gas producers, who measure and constrain their daily production to control supply and price, Russia produces all it can to gobble as much market share as possible. In fact, Russia swaggered as the leading oil producer in the world, outpacing Saudi Arabia, until being dethroned by the unrestrained and aggressive energy policy of the Trump administration.

Under Trump, America became the globe's number one producer, achieving both long-sought domestic energy independence and expanding into export markets. This remaking of the oil supply lines has dramatically reshaped the petropolitics of the Middle East, facilitating the summer 2020 peace treaties between Israel and Gulf states such as the United Arab Emirates and Bahrain. This process has blunted the effects of Russian proxy wars and destabilization tactics. But this has not deterred Russia from meddling through other vectors.

Russian's foreign policy is bold and militarized. Moscow took over Crimea and has made embattled Syria a vassal. Likewise, Moscow intimidates the Ukraine and other parts of eastern Europe. Russia is also adept at the cyberwarfare; however, it is facing a demographic challenge: its population is contracting. Of its population of 145 million, 20 percent are Muslims. This percentage is growing fast there, as it is elsewhere. The larger Russian population still suffers from the national generation-to-generation consequences of excessive vodka consumption. Its inadequate healthcare system limits Russians' average longevity to only 60–65 years, far below the 75-year level of the US and most Western countries. Within 50 years, if not effectively managed, Russia could become a Muslim-majority country. The Muslim population has been growing at three to five percent annually, while the Russian Christian population has been falling by one percent annually. This dilemma might partially explain Russia's desire to influence and dominate Europe, and even reconstitute the Soviet Union.

Just because a nation is led by a dictator does not mean it cannot host robust capitalism. Both China and Russia are dictatorships, running highly centralized governments largely managed by crony capitalists. They use capitalism as a tool in their arsenals as they challenge democracies, both ours and others in the world.

However, Russian capitalism suffers from its legacy of communism and Stalinism. It still has not learned how to harness its innovative scientists, engineers, and entrepreneurs nearly as well as the US, Europe, and Israel have.

On the other hand, China has learned how to invest and become innovative. Still, the country is particularly plagued by out-of-control water and air pollution. Poorly controlled environmental carcinogens are boosting cancer rates by 5–10 percent annually. This continues to affect a national population still reeling from fifty years of the state-imposed one-child policy. China's national and local debt is officially nearly three hundred percent of its GDP—triple that of the United

States. Unofficially, China's total government debt may well be 400–600 percent of its GDP.

Unlike Islamist entities, with whom negotiations are impossible, strategic competitors such as Russia and China can and should be engaged through the negotiating process. However, such negotiations are fruitless unless backed by strong US military capabilities.

During the past twenty-five years, Russia and China have only half-joined Western civilization. True, they have adopted many Western values; they should be encouraged to adopt more such values. Like other civilized countries, Russia and China are threatened by political Islam. This means they need help—and that help can come from Washington under the right circumstances. Our cooperation must go hand in hand with encouraging them—and eventually compelling them—to abandon their evil allies, such as Iran, North Korea, Cuba, and Venezuela.

Economic sanctions are the first step to curb the power of this new axis of evil; but eventually, such measures must be made crippling, backed up by the selective use of military force. Western civilization is not safe without regime change in those countries run by the forces of evil.

Communist China has a goal. By 2049, the hundredth anniversary of the Communist revolution, China seeks to be the predominant economic power, that is, the center axis of the world, replacing the United States and Europe. China has withstood continuous challenges from within and from outsiders throughout its five thousand years of recorded history. It therefore possesses the patience to succeed in the long term, while the US focuses on short-term solutions it thinks will solve long-term challenges.

Russia knows the agony of war and destruction. For generations, it suffered under bitter winters of starvation and czarist suppression. During WWI, Russia lost two million men, more than any other nation. In the years between the wars, Stalin instituted a reign of terror and manipulation exceeding anything Europe had seen before. During WWII, the Nazis burned and starved cities; by the time Berlin finally succumbed in May 1945, some 17 million Russian civilians and combatants had perished. In other words, Russia lost fifteen percent of its population in less than half a decade. Russia then continued the war within its own borders, imprisoning and starving millions. Of the estimated 18 million that were exiled into cruel gulags, almost ten percent perished under ghastly conditions.

Both China and Russia know the rigors of a multifront war. They have endured it in prior centuries and have learned to wage it in the present century. America has yet to discern its multifront war, let alone wage it.

Chapter Nine: The Rise of the Radical Left in the US

Most Americans do not understand that we are already in the midst of a true civil war. At stake are our freedoms and way of life. Political correctness, socialism, progressivism, and Islamism have greatly influenced our political leaders, aided by the left wing's captive media and entertainment industry. Many Democrats push this agenda; most Republicans fail to counter it. The ninety-year-old Muslim Brotherhood and other Islamist entities have succeeded in penetrating and influencing both national parties via political contributions.

Americans are their own worst enemies. In the third quarter of 2016, at the end of the Obama administration, the US military was funded at a level of only three to four percent of the GDP, reducing its ability to simultaneously fight two—or even one and a half—major conventional wars. We were also incapable of waging simultaneous asymmetric wars in some two to three dozen hotspots of the world, where US interests, as well as Christian minority populations and our vulnerable allies, must be defended.

Jews can also be their own worst enemies. Close to half of all American Jews actively support anti-Jewish and anti-Israel organizations such as J Street, the New Israel Fund, and Jewish Voice for Peace. These groups undermine the Jewish State and the US–Israel alliance. Many in the Jewish community believe that the old-line, mainstream Jewish organizations, such as the American Israel Political Action Committee (AIPAC) and the Anti-Defamation League (ADL), long ago failed in their primary missions.

More to the point, about seventy percent of Jews still support the Democratic Party, which increasingly tolerates left-wing, antisemitic, anti-Zionist, and racist voices. Among these are the four members of the US House of Representatives known as "The Squad." Individually, they are Representatives Rashida Tlaib (D-MI), Ayanna Pressley (D-MA), Ilhan Omar (D-MN), and their nominal leader, Alexandria Ocasio-Cortez (D-NY). While it may seem like the Squad is just four representatives scattered across the country, a surging movement of liberal, socialist, and anti-Israel politicians is joining their ranks, running for office, and supporting openly socialist candidates. More than that, these four wield an outsized power within the Democratic Party. They pursue a radical agenda, including defunding police, boycotting Israel, and opposing American foreign policy accomplishments.

The election of Barack Obama as president for the second time demonstrated that America's Judeo-Christian values and culture have failed to stand up to the false narratives of political correctness from the left and from political Islam. Mr. Obama came to the fore with a far-left background, open to Islamist dogma. Moreover, he was totally unprepared for such a job, having never managed a company or organization of any consequence. His main credential was disrupting the existing order through community activism.

True to form, the Obama administration and Congress enacted socialist legislation such as the Affordable Care Act (ACA), nationalization of student loan debt, and in 2010, the Dodd-Frank banking controls. These pieces of legislation are good examples of short-term popular actions that derailed the long-term growth rate of the GDP.

During eight years of liberal or progressive or socialist governance in the Saul Alinsky tradition, the federal government accelerated its assumption of extra powers. Alinsky was the author of *Rules for Radicals*, a book that set forth game plans for mobilizing "have-nots" in order to deconstruct and reconstruct the system. Furthermore, the Democratic Party, taken over by radicals beginning in the 1960s, is now receptive to the false narratives of both socialism and Islamism, two movements that have become fellow traveling partners despite their divergent origins. Also, new groups, such as the Democratic Socialists of America and the Justice Democrats are attempting to further radicalize the Democratic Party from within.

The Obama administration's mismanagement caused the annual GDP growth rate to slow to just under two percent—well below the traditional three to four percent growth that could have occurred with proper economic management. The lack of true growth was exacerbated by the Treasury and Justice Departments' war on banks and financial institutions, as well as various agencies'—the CFPB, the EPA, the NLRB, and the SEC— regulatory war on businesses.

The Obama administration, like its predecessor, encouraged Sharia-compliant financial institutions to operate and expand in the US. Sharia-compliant financing was invented decades ago by the Muslim Brotherhood to dictate how investors make contributions to Islamic charities (*zakat*); but it is actually of deeper Islamic origin, with rules governing the lending of money, as well as investment profit and loss. Today, zakat contributions are allocated by special imams, who are hired by banks to promote Sharia, often through the Muslim Brotherhood. Zakat often lacks transparency; this is in violation of US non-profit laws, which limit charitable donations for political purposes. This advancement of politics from within religious organizations violates the separation of church and state but is still commonplace among a range of religious groups. President Trump inadvertently exacerbated this situation through a recent executive order advising the IRS to be lenient toward political activity by religious organizations.

The Muslim Brotherhood movement grew out of two major Sunni branches, one from Egypt and a somewhat smaller branch from Pakistan (*Tablighi Jama'at*). Today, the Brotherhood's foremost supporters are Turkey, Qatar, and even the revolutionary Shiite regime in Iran. It has been successful in penetrating our political systems, schools, media, and entertainment industry through the creation of many front or allied Muslim organizations. They can be found operating from the campus to the community. These organizations gain power through character assassination, the suppression of free speech, and lawfare—invoking false claims of Islamophobia. Behind these complaints always lies the threat of violence. University administrators are quick to comply with Islamists' demands, thus abdicating their duty to protect the rights of all their students.

The Brotherhood's ideology is the intellectual force behind political Islam. The group even produced a document, titled "An Explanatory Memorandum," delineating its plan to conquer the US. This document was entered into evidence in both the famous "Holyland Foundation" terrorism trial and a 2016 Senate investigative hearing. Produced by the Muslim Brotherhood in North America, the document states unambiguously: "The process of settlement is a 'Civilization-Jihadist Process' with all the word means. The Ikhwan (fighting soldiers) must understand that their work in America is a kind of grand Jihad in eliminating and destroying Western civilization from within and 'sabotaging' its miserable house by their hands and the hands of the believers so that it is eliminated, and God's religion is made victorious over all other religions."

The Muslim Brotherhood has also succeeded in proselytizing its version of Islam throughout federal and state prison systems, as well as US military and security services. Separate from the MB, the Nation of Islam has even received federal financing for its prison-based ministry—or indoctrination. This outreach policy, known as *Da'wa*, has become increasingly successful by providing social and financial support to new adherents.

America and the West have yet to develop a cohesive strategy for defeating political Islam. We are hindered by moral relativism, which masks reality. We thereby blind ourselves and hamper our ability to defend ourselves and defeat our enemies. Such moral relativism is often promoted by our schools, media, TV shows, and Hollywood.

America's media outlets have collectively failed to protect our culture by perpetuating the false narratives of our enemies. They disseminate disinformation, broadly lambasted as fake news, while playing on the audience's emotions. While the term "fake news" is relatively new, the concept is well-established in America's media history. It is taught in most high school history classes as "yellow journalism." A chief exponent of yellow journalism was William Randolph Hearst, who famously quipped, "You furnish the pictures and I'll furnish the war," as he was fomenting US involvement in Cuba.

In the minds of many, the yellow journalism tradition of Hearst newspapers and even Henry Ford's infamous *The Dearborn Independent* is now perpetuated by CNN and MSNBC. These are outstanding examples of outlets that ill-inform the public. The *New York Times*, *The Washington Post*, and *The Huffington Post* are but a few of the outlets constantly accused of proliferating misinformation. These media giants have proven particularly adept at smearing those perceived as political and intellectual enemies.

The entertainment industry repeatedly promotes anti-Americanism to the unsuspecting public, directly harming the country. It is also guilty of mischaracterizing political Islam, directly or indirectly, by its unwillingness to address the issue objectively.

Both free expression and freedom of the press are enshrined in the First Amendment to the US Constitution. This freedom, unique to America, is being abused to promote the fake news which has permeated our airwaves, internet sites, and newspaper stands. Tech giants such as Facebook, Wikipedia, YouTube, Google, LinkedIn, and Twitter have adopted reviewing policies that entail political correctness, a standard that curtails our freedom of expression and hampers criticism and exposure of our enemies. Yet, at the same time, social media and leading Internet sites allow leftist and Islamist hate, as well as racist and violence-promoting messages, to spread like a pandemic without a vaccine. In 2020, Twitter explained that it would censor President Trump for so-called hate content, but it permits the ayatollahs in Iran to use its platform to deny the Holocaust, threaten the destruction of Tel Aviv, and call for death to America and Israel.

Major internet providers are refusing to close down rogue sites—right-wing and left-wing—that promote hate speech and violence. Some have even teamed up with organizations such as the Southern Poverty Law Center (SPLC) and Muslim Brotherhood-affiliated groups that mischaracterize pro-American and pro-Western organizations as "hate organizations." This devious tactic projects the values of evil onto the forces of good, thereby confusing the average citizen.

Internet companies should be held accountable and penalized by our legal system. Yet, there has been no cohesive response to these attacks on the American way of life and values. Such a daunting challenge seems beyond the abilities of our politicians. The Trump administration seems still unable to change the false narrative. Instead, Obama administration leftovers are free to continue anti-American propaganda. To correct the situation, wealthy Americans should invest in alternative, pro-American media outlets so that Americans can be accurately informed, enabling them to discern and disregard false narratives.

Until the moment America can foster media reform, the nation will not be able to act wisely or with acuity in its multifront war.

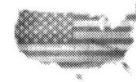

Chapter Ten: Defeating Political Islam

Today, Christians are the largest persecuted minority in the world. This is a major concern for the survival of Western civilization; this concern is greatly heightened by Christian leaders' apparent lack of understanding of political Islam.

Pope Francis has repeatedly declared that Islam and Christianity are similar in their pursuit of peace. Not surprisingly, in 2017, Francis legitimized Palestinian radicalism by granting the "Palestinian state" an embassy in the Vatican City State. Pope Francis publicly condemned the persecution of Muslims in Myanmar by Buddhists but said nothing about Christian persecution by Muslims. Pope Francis and other Christian leaders also argue that it is unfair to equate Islamist jihadists with terrorism. So, what chance do Christians have in Muslim-majority countries where jihadists are regularly killing in the name of Islam? Why are Western Christian leaders mum when Christians are being killed for their faith? To stop the killings there should be an effort to reform Islam. It is necessary to separate politics from religion.

Islam, like Christianity and Judaism, is an Abrahamic religion. But Islamism is different. Rather than coexisting with other faiths, Islamism considers Sharia superior to other legal systems and seeks to implement it everywhere by any means. Political Islam seeks to dictate not only religious interpretations of the

Quran and the Hadith but also the political, social, cultural, economic, and military behavior of Muslims and non-Muslims everywhere. Judaism, Christianity, and other religions celebrate life. Islam celebrates death, to quote Islamist leaders. But some brave Muslim reformers have been trying to bridge the gap, calling for the separation of mosque and state.

Reformers face a set of difficulties and regular threats from Islamic orthodoxy; moreover, they are mostly ignored by Western leaders. Former President Barack Hussein Obama and Canadian Prime Minister Justin Trudeau exacerbated the problem by endorsing the Muslim Brotherhood's agenda. Yet, many Muslim nations, such as Egypt, Saudi Arabia, and the UAE, have banned the MB. Egyptian President Abdel Fattah el-Sisi has been leading the charge. In the West, a few individual brave voices, such as former Somali-Dutch parliamentarian Ayaan Hirsi Ali, and moderate commentators, such as Zuhdi Jasser, Raymond Ibrahim, Noni Darwish, and others are calling out for reform.

Yet, non-Muslim Western voices calling for Islamic reform are being shunned by the progressive left, mischaracterized, ostracized, and threatened. A good example is the trials and tribulations of brave Dutch parliamentary reformer Geert Wilders and the French satirical magazine *Charlie Hebdo*, whose offices were attacked by al-Qaeda terrorists in 2015—killing a dozen people—for publishing a set of cartoons of Mohammed, the founder of Islam. The magazine office's former location was attacked again in September 2020 by a Pakistani jihadist wielding a meat cleaver. He wounded two people. French police arrested six accomplices, and

Interior Minister Gérald Darmanin stated this was "clearly an act of Islamist terrorism."

Western leaders should actively support Muslims who seek to reform Islam. Countries with Muslim majorities should also move toward separating religion from politics; this would immediately lessen their internal and external tensions. It would also contribute to deterring those who practice political Islam from creating alternative societies aimed at undermining Western-style democracies. If this is not done, Western democracies will be devastated in 25–50 years.

The West could emerge victorious—but only with a proper winning strategy. For now, Western leaders do not seem to fully understand the threats posed by mass migration of Muslims to their countries. This replacement ethos undermines nations' economic, cultural, and physical existence. Besides, population growth is slowing in Western countries other than Israel. Family formation is falling to 1.2 to 1.8 children per family unit, depending upon the country. This is well below the replacement rate of 2.1. Furthermore, the growing socialist movement both here and abroad is demanding more benefits for their declining populations.

Because of their growing challenges, Western-style nations are not easy for the average person to comprehend. We should begin by exposing the Islamist movement—and banning it, as many nations have done with Nazis. This counter-offensive should begin now. There must be no compromise with political Islam. Time is one of their tactics.

Western nations must resolve to protect Christians worldwide, with or without the help of organized church bodies such as the Vatican. The US, the leader of the free world, with a population that is ninety percent Christian, should not stand by and watch Christians be massacred. Before long, the Trump administration must create a comprehensive strategy to aid and save Christians worldwide. This strategy should utilize a variety of elements, including economic sanctions against nations where minority Christian populations are threatened.

Our national security plan to win the war against the Islamists must also include a strategy for defeating the Islamic Republic of Iran, which supports global terror organizations with many thousands of agents and operatives, all working to undermine their host countries and Western civilization as a whole. But none of these defense stratagems, from religious reform to banishment of the most threatening of political entities, can work if we do not refocus our view of the multifront war.

Chapter Eleven: Solving Problems, Implementing Solutions

The collective challenges facing the US, Europe, and Israel are the same. First, our economies have been historically underperforming, with only one to two percent annual growth instead of a consistent, healthy two to four percent. Second, our constitutional and religious freedoms and our secular culture are being undermined by false narratives, political correctness, and censorship. Third, we all lack cybersecurity and physical protection, including safeguards for critical infrastructure such as the electrical grid.

Americans have lost control over their educational system. Most public school curricula have been corrupted by political correctness and PC shaming. The Obama administration extended federal control and mandated false narratives to states and local school systems. The teaching of Western civilization, history, and civics has been neglected. Students are not encouraged to analyze problems and develop their thinking and problem-solving skills. Yet many of the new curricula include Muslim Brotherhood false narratives. Under President Obama, the federal government nationalized the student loan program and encouraged students to take on extra debt, which is forgiven only for those who subsequently go to work for the government.

Public school teacher unions consistently resist vouchers for private and charter schools, thereby forcing students to remain in failing schools. The unions represent the interests of the teachers, not the students or parents; therefore, parents must reassert their rights and the rights of their children.

European countries have abdicated their responsibility to protect their nation-states economically, culturally, and physically, and most have not produced real economic growth over the past fifteen years. Europe has abdicated its Judeo-Christian religious history and its secular culture in favor of political correctness in the deluded hope that it can coexist with political Islam. At the same time, overly generous welfare benefits are sapping economic growth, which reduces Europe's ability to fund national security and contributes to increased immigration from Africa and the Middle East. Most European countries have cut their national defense spending to an anemic one to two percent of their GDPs. With such anemic funding, NATO can neither protect Europe from Russia outside its borders nor Islamic terrorism and political Islam within its borders. Time is running out for Europe to save itself.

Solutions for the US, Europe, and Israel should begin by re-affirming Judeo-Christian and related Western values of representative democracy. All must lift restraints on economic growth. Concomitant with financial strength, there must come the strengthening of social institutions. Europe should remember the Calvinists. During the eighteenth and nineteenth centuries, especially as it flourished in the Netherlands, Calvinism held individuals responsible for their behavior while ensuring individual rights and tolerance for minorities.

Europe must particularly learn the lesson of formerly majority-Christian Lebanon, a land where Jesus walked, and Christianity established one of its earliest anchors. But over the centuries, Lebanon failed to protect its Christian population. It did not curb the Muslim invasion after it was abandoned by the French in 1955. As a result, during the past fifty years, the Christian population has declined from sixty percent to about forty percent today. No one knows for sure, because since 1937, Lebanon has been unwilling to organize a national census. Today, some Christians in Lebanon behave as dhimmis, as if the nation were under Muslim control, while others feel compelled to fight for survival. Unless dramatic changes occur, within another fifty years, there may be no substantial Christian community left in Lebanon.

Apply the lessons of Lebanon to Europe: In fifty to seventy-five years, there may be no Christians in Holland or Belgium. In a century, there may be no Christians in major countries such as the UK, France, and Germany. Alternatively, these nations might split up into autonomous areas. Many of these countries risk becoming victims of their own potential two-state solutions. The development of autonomous areas will almost certainly be advanced by the growth of ethnically contentious zones such as we see even now.

Fortifying internally will not be successful unless each European nation dramatically improves its cybersecurity, which is required to protect both critical and non-critical infrastructure.

Likewise, the US federal government must restructure and downsize. President Trump's announcement of a governmental hiring freeze is a good start, but an overhaul is long overdue. America deserves a depoliticized and merit-based civil service. Reform will only begin when current employees are replaced by new hires of high talent and the old Obama and Clinton-sponsored employees fired. In other words, the deep state must be removed. Anti-American and politicized bureaucrats, to the maximum extent legally possible, should be sent packing. How can this be done without resembling a purge? A business-like makeover would ensure that people are not removed except for cause, including lack of performance, and except for political conduct. We can never allow personal preference or belief to be considered—as is done in many state, local, and federal positions after every election. People should keep their politics to themselves. So long as the government workplace is politics-free and merit-based, America can advance.

National laws forbidding the sale and use of illicit drugs must be enforced. Illicit drugs destroy the brain and harm the body. Too often, they render our citizens incapable of enjoying a healthy personal life and achieving economic success. Drugged-out people too often become a burden to society. Marijuana should remain illegal except for research and medicinal use. There is enough scientific evidence showing the long-term harm caused by using marijuana for recreational purposes.

The K–12 educational system must be reformed through state-by-state liberalization of education savings accounts (ESAs). State governments, subsidized by the federal government, have proven themselves to be unreliable and untrustworthy regarding our children. State and local governments have increasingly ceded control of textbooks to the false narratives of the socialist–Islamist alliance. Teacher tenure rules must be restructured or eliminated. Charter schools must be expanded dramatically. For post-schooling workers, we must consolidate and upgrade our worker retraining programs to offset the challenges of proliferating industrial automation. On the university level, the federal government should use its funding clout to insist that academic faculties maintain a diversity of opinion, not just a diversity of gender and skin color.

The US must regain legal control over non-profit organizations and especially non-governmental organizations (NGOs) that pretend to be charities but are politically active. Taxpayers subsidize all such tax-exempt entities. Thus, we all end up financing movements anathema to our way of life. We must eliminate the not-for-profit tax status of NGOs that engage in political activity.

The US must take control over all of its borders. The country must reform legal immigration laws and prevent illegal immigration. We must end the family unification program (chain migration) and the diversity lottery system. The Diversity Immigrant Visa Program (DV Program) normally allots some fifty thousand immigrant visas annually to a random selection of individuals from countries which ordinarily show a low rate of immigration to America. We must particularly learn how to implement extreme vetting to eliminate both cultural and physical threats. Newly developed suspect detection systems must be utilized. From the outset—that is, even before they first set foot on US soil—all new immigrants must pledge allegiance to our values and the Constitution before entry is allowed. They should be required to repeat the process before Permanent Resident (Green) Cards are issued and before citizenship is granted. Those who violate their pledges or commit crimes should be deported. The suite of reforms should include an E-Verify system and US citizenship ID cards for employment, entitlements, safety net programs, and voting. Employers who knowingly hire illegal immigrants should be punished as harshly as those workers—especially if those employers provided falsified employment eligibility documentation.

Subversive Islamist organizations should be kept at bay, as communists were during the Cold War and American Nazis were during WWII. The CIA must reinvigorate its human intelligence (HUMINT) abilities. Domestic security and law enforcement agencies must expand their focus to include both physical and cultural terror organizations. These agencies are not properly configured to tackle political Islam. Both have been penetrated by adherents of the Muslim Brotherhood and other Islamist organizations. The State Department should be reinfused with unambiguously pro-American officers. As always, such reforms must be undertaken deftly to advance the primacy of our values without undermining our precious personal liberties—otherwise, we risk ourselves having accomplished the goal of those who target our freedoms.

We must also move all of our bases out of MB-influenced countries such as Turkey and Qatar. We should negotiate new bases or enlarge existing ones in friendly and freedom-loving countries, such as Cyprus, Greece, Italy, or India, to preserve our ability to project power and rapidly respond around the world. That said, military postures, advancing technologies, and asymmetric forces are rapidly changing the very character of military power. Hypersonic warfare, the newly announced Space Force, nano warfare, energy dynamics, material science, EMP cyberwarfare, artificial intelligence, robotics, drones, and laser weaponry are all redefining the next generations of military power. Here, Israel and the United States excel.

China is, however, nipping at our scientific heels, especially in the realm of nano warfare and the creation of militarized artificial islands in disputed waters. Vibro-compaction of dredged sands makes viable land where none had existed. Many urban planners in dozens of countries have created artificial islands for peaceful purposes, such as airports and urban expansion. It is China that has taken these techniques to the next level as a vehicle for hegemony and military intimidation.

In Latin America, the US must revive the Monroe Doctrine. The Monroe Doctrine was announced in 1823 by President James Monroe; it was designed to protect North America from the threat of European colonialization in South America. In the 1950s and 1960s, the Monroe Doctrine focused on protecting Latin America from communist infiltration. Now, the principles of this doctrine must be refocused on protecting our southern neighbors from infiltration by Turkey, Iran, and Islamist organizations. Even now, Turkey and Iran are influencing Latin America, especially Venezuela, Nicaragua, El Salvador, and Cuba. Iran controls over eighty cultural centers throughout Latin America; these conduct a cultural war against Christian populations. After decades of purposeful infiltration, Iran has now embedded tens of thousands of agents, operatives, cultural terrorists, narco-terrorists, and physical terrorists throughout Latin America. The US government should assist Latin American governments in properly defining cultural and physical terror organizations and then declaring them illegal. Iran is now using its successful Latin American penetration model to invade Africa.

Regarding China, we must continue to challenge this highly confident, 5,000-year-old civilization on numerous fronts. We must succeed in renegotiating our trade relationship to eliminate unfair, unilateral, and often illegal technology transfer, as well as the theft of intellectual property. We must close all of China's Confucius Institutes on our college campuses. Also, we must lead with our values, rebuild our infrastructure, reorganize our government, and insist on an international order based on freedom. In sum, we must create a national strategy to confront China in our ongoing society-on-society competition.

In Europe, the US must facilitate Brexit with improved trade status for the UK and its former commonwealth countries. Ireland should also be encouraged to join this alliance because it shares a common border. If Ireland remains in the EU, this may undermine the UK's immigration policies and ultimately its security. Brexit would allow the UK to reset its immigration policy to keep out migrants that do not believe in the common law of the land. If the UK does not take this opportunity to regain control over its immigration process, the Brexit effort will be moot. The UK should look at Australia's policy of encouraging the assimilation of immigrants combined with the deportation of those unwilling to accept its laws and values.

The non-homogeneous nature of Europe makes it more difficult to implement appropriate solutions. Individual countries should reclaim their sovereignty from the failed EU bureaucracy. A better future awaits Eastern European countries that suffered 45 years under Soviet communism. Poland, Hungary, Slovakia, and the Czech Republic are maintaining their cultural cohesion and holding fast to their existing legal modalities by not accepting mass migrations of young

Muslim men from the Middle East or Africa. It is not the same for Western European countries, which are now undergoing an invasion of newcomers with ideologies contrary to Western values. In the absence of a concerted counter-strategy, the Muslim population in most Western European countries is projected to rise from 7–10 percent in 2018 to 25–45 percent by 2050. But those percentages belie facts on the ground. In some countries, regions, and cities, the influx is now so great that the term "Eurabia" is bandied about with both levity and dread.

We must immediately enable NATO to contend with political Islam. A properly-sized NATO navy should immediately blockade illegal migrants from Africa and Turkey. Virtually all of this migration is accomplished through human trafficking along modern slave routes. That will not be easy, as Standing NATO Maritime Group One is a poorly-equipped token fleet. This means NATO members will have to create a multi-national fleet as they have done to combat piracy, smuggling, and terrorism. Today, Combined Task Force 150 operates against pirates, terrorists, and smugglers, interdicting suspect vessels every day. Its 33-nation coalition headquarters is in Bahrain. Australia also has experience in intercepting human traffickers, ensuring their boats do not reach the shores Down Under.

In the longer term, Europe must seek ways to help improve economic development in Africa and the Middle East to reduce unemployment there, which drives the resulting migration of the youth. Particular help should be forthcoming to the Christian population in Africa in its fight for survival against radical Muslims. Several African countries—Rwanda, Chad, and Mali—have recently shown some encouraging signs, such as closer cooperation with Israel. Angola has taken steps to ensure that its small Islamic community does not proselytize or become a magnet for an influx of foreign Muslims, but has been targeted by oft-debunked false claims that Islam had been banned and mosques destroyed.

The European Union should return to its original mission of promoting trade—and get out of politics. The European Commission must be reorganized from an essentially unelected proxy government into a free trade union. The EU has failed to grow its economy, protect the culture of its member states, and protect its people physically. The EU also failed to protect its members during the COVID-19 pandemic of 2020. It has lost its right to rule. Thus, sovereignty must be returned to individual countries. What Brexit did for Great Britain is now a growing trend in other countries such as where Euroskeptics have created the Italeave movement in Italy and Nexit in the Netherlands.

The Jewish state of Israel has been fighting for its existence since its establishment. Israel, a small and homogeneous country with a long history of challenges, is ironically the best-positioned Western-aligned country to solve its major problems. Since 1948, Israel has been in a continuous state of war, far longer than any country in existence today. Thus, Israel has had to spend at least six to eight percent of its GDP on its national security, which in turn has enabled it to build, relative to its size, the strongest internal security and external military power in the world.

For Israel to continue to exist as a Jewish state, the government must regain control over its educational system. The State directly or indirectly supports four educational structures: ultra-orthodox Jewish; modern Orthodox Jewish; secular Jewish; and Muslim and Christian-Arab. Only thirty percent of the common curriculum is shared by all. Ultra-orthodox Jews do not learn enough math and science, while secular Jews do not learn enough history and religion, and Arabs do not learn enough Hebrew, English, or science. Only the modern Orthodox in Israel teach a balanced curriculum.

The government must also regain control over its legal system, which is being undermined by excessively leftist and activist Supreme Court justices who routinely overrule decisions of the elected Knesset. Unlike in the US, Israeli justices are presented for nomination by a committee dominated by the justices themselves. To improve its Supreme Court, Israel should adopt the US tradition of having justices nominated by the Prime Minister. Otherwise, ultra-liberal Israeli justices will eternally replace themselves with ideologues who share their mindset.

Israel must also finally extend sovereignty to Area B and half of Area C and its 150 communities, which comprise about 9 percent of Judea and Samaria. These areas, created by the Oslo Accords, affect half a million Israeli citizens. When implemented, this change will leave Area A, which is populated by Arabs, under military-civil administration until the PA ceases its war against Israel. Full sovereignty over Areas B and C will allow Israel to protect the land from the current invasion by the PA and EU-financed squatters. In the interim, Israel should accept the Trump administration's plan—the so-called Deal of the Century.

The three strongholds of Western civilization and liberty—the United States, Europe, and Israel—can survive as bastions of our joint values, but only if they implement multifront solutions for a multifront war.

Chapter Twelve: COVID-19's Consequences

The novel coronavirus SARS-CoV2, which causes the illness known as COVID-19, began spreading around the world in December 2019 after several months of contagion largely confined to Wuhan province. The tragic numbers of COVID-19 change by the day. At the time of this writing, early October 2020, the WHO reports that more than 35 million people have been infected, and more than a million have died. More than 26 million people have recovered in more than 200 countries and territories around the world, but among those recovered are the "long-haulers," whose recoveries are far from complete. In the US, the virus has infected more than 7.5 million people and killed more than 208,000. By the time these words are read, the tallies are predicted to be much higher.

However, the true numbers may never be known. The Chinese government's dubious September 19, 2020 report claimed only 85,372 cases since the outbreak with only 4,634 deaths. It is also nearly certain that Iran, North Korea, Myanmar, and Russia, believed to be major hot spots, have vastly under-reported their numbers. Many African nations have poor reporting procedures, so an entire continent may be under-reporting its numbers. Just as it took us years to assess the true figures for the Black Death and the

1918 influenza pandemic, it may take a generation before true data are assembled.

Experts—and a gamut of informed speculation—differ on the origin of COVID-19. But the most commonly held view is that the virus originated at the Wuhan Institute of Virology, where China researches biological weapons. It is unclear whether the virus escaped from the lab by accident. However, there is no doubt that the Chinese authorities hid the details of this virus outbreak for at least two months—November and December 2019—thereby causing a devastating pandemic at a time when days mattered.

Who will be hurt the most? Let us look at the virus's potential to harm democracies or hybrid democracies that cover half of the world's population vs. authoritarian regimes, which rule the remainder. Dictatorships, which cover up their failures, will be hurt far more in the long term due to greater economic contraction. All nations have already suffered a reduction of ten to thirty percent in economic growth. Almost all have already announced crash programs to develop new vaccines and therapeutics and are trying to quarantine the vulnerable and infectious segments of their populations.

Within a year or two of the virus's appearance, democracies will far outshine dictatorships. Democracies are full of highly-capable private sector healthcare companies, which adapt rapidly to challenges through new drugs, new vaccines, new diagnostic tests, expanded emergency rooms, well-stocked pharmacies, hospitals with extensive safety protocols, with an emphasis on domestic production and services that will be delivered in a safer, decentralized manner. Because of their sophisticated healthcare delivery systems, democracies are expected to experience far lower mortality rates and improved outcomes for those who recover.

Meanwhile, dictatorships, especially China, will likely see a massive slowdown in their annual economic growth rates, from six percent growth to perhaps as much as a five percentage points less than that for the early quarters of the second year of the virus. In the longer term, manufacturing plants will suffer for years as customers diversify outside of China. Pharmaceutical marketers will move from manufacturers in China to those in India, Vietnam, as well as back to the US. Puerto Rico, wracked by bad tax and other economic policies and pummeled by hurricanes, has already been positioned by the White House in late 2020 to recover its former primacy in pharmaceutical manufacturing; the global shift, however, will take years.

Iran's economy has fallen by as much as five percent and could fall further, by as much as ten percent annually for several years to come. This type of contraction might hasten the demise of the corrupt theocrats who rule the Islamic Republic. Qatar, Venezuela, and Russia, all heavily dependent on income from oil production, will be hurt badly by the thirty to fifty percent decline in oil prices due to slower worldwide economic growth and lockdown measures. Russia has demonstrated a dismal record of responding to public health and safety emergencies. The debacle at Chernobyl and the needless loss of the submarine *Kursk* are just two of many examples of how the Russian bureaucracy foolishly hides disasters and mismanages its responses.

Dictatorships also face the problem of rising social unrest among their young people, who are tired of high unemployment and slow economic growth. Restive populations realize that squandered resources could have been used to dramatically upgrade the healthcare systems in their nations and protect their lives. This applies additional pressure on the typical dictatorship's quest to maintain the high military expenditures required to fight wars.

The COVID-19 pandemic represents an existential threat to the leaders of the dictatorial Iranian regime, as its population has witnessed their leaders' incompetence in handling this medical and public health emergency. Their modest resources continue to be wasted fighting endless wars in foreign lands for the purpose of spreading political Islam worldwide. This could lead to toppling the mullahs in Tehran, whose power is tenuously held together by corrupt police, brutal paramilitaries, and loyal military forces. Were the theocratic regime to fall, a weakened Iran might be unable to sustain its expensive support of the narco-dictatorship of Venezuela. This would, in turn, enable the restive population there to overthrow the corrupt regime of Nicolás Maduro, who was indicted by the US for drug trafficking. The same process may soon be apparent for the Houthi rebels in Yemen, Hamas terrorists in Gaza, Hezbollah militants in Lebanon, and multiple fighting units throughout Syria.

Surviving the darkness of the pandemic, Western civilization will shine despite a plethora of near-term challenges. Democracies and their free markets are the fountains of innovation in the world, driving future prosperity. Properly managed democracies will recover within a year or two, while dictatorships will be far more challenged, with the possible exception of China and North Korea, which have both achieved a draconian level of social oppression designed to overwhelm any hint of dissatisfaction, let alone an uprising.

International supra-organizations will also be impacted—and it will not be just the EU. The United Nations and its related organizations, particularly the World Health Organization, have failed to play a useful role in the pandemic. A move to replace or greatly restructure them will arise.

Even seemingly unrelated entities such as the International Criminal Court (ICC) and the UNRWA will be greatly undermined as cash from governments and confidence from the populace at large continue to shrink. The ICC has failed to act on what many have called a crime against humanity: China's unleashing of its virus. UNRWA has failed in its mission to superintend the health and welfare of hundreds of thousands under its care in Gaza and elsewhere in the Middle East. The agency has demonstrated the bankruptcy of wasting millions during an active movement of terror and diplomatic combat. In the end, UNRWA was left with rhetoric, wasted resources, and a massive infection rate among the people it supposedly looks after.

COVID-19 and its consequences will undoubtedly change the world as we know it, in ways subtle and profound. Beyond its social and economic implications, the pandemic has injected a powerful disruptor into the waging of the multifront war.

Chapter Thirteen: Winning the Multifront War

The strategies presented here may help us survive and thrive over the next half century, but only if we fully confront our multiple enemies. The challenges we face are multidimensional in structure and cannot be resolved solely by military means. The military is organized through the integration of the resources of the Army, Navy, Air Force, Marines, Coast Guard, and the new Space Force. However, our military abilities must also be integrated with all the other forms of warfare and defense: cultural, economic, legal, and demographic. Only a multidisciplinary strategy of integration can succeed, one that combines all aspects of our governmental and private sector resources. Only then we can prevail in what many call the clash of civilizations. If we are to save Western civilization, we must immediately implement a concerted, proactive strategy to disarm the socialist–Islamist alliance. We must ensure that we do not repeat mistakes made by once-Christian countries such as Egypt, what is now Turkey, Morocco, Syria, and Lebanon. Their mistakes were: not growing their economies, not protecting their cultures, and failing to win their wars of defense against Muslim invaders. The invaders of prior centuries are the majorities that occupy these lands today.

Greatly impeding our ability to win is the rapid growth of the resistance that began about four years ago with the election of President Trump and which has been exacerbated by disruptions by the Deep State as well as the indirect takeover of the Democratic party by such radicals as the Socialist Workers Party, Democratic Socialists of America, the Communist Party, and the Justice Democrats. All these radical parties combined have historically garnered a small percentage of the vote. But they have discovered they no longer need to build a base. They can hijack an existing base.

The coalition of socialist and Islamist forces is working hard to stave off defeat by Constitution-revering conservatives. This coalition is also trying to corrupt the election process by nationalizing the electoral process, which is constitutionally reserved to states and localities. Behind the coalition are numerous globalist, anti-American think tanks, such as George Soros's Open Society Foundations and their affiliates.

Physical enemies require physical solutions. No known effective non-military deterrent exists for Iran, ISIS, al-Qaeda, Hezbollah, Boko Haram, or the Taliban. World War II should be a great reminder of what happens when the forces of good do not confront the forces of evil early on. How many millions lost their lives because of miscalculation, procrastination, and accommodation?

It seems that the lessons of appeasement and immobility were in some ways relearned during the Cold War. Peace through strength policies ultimately won the day. Going forward, an economically, culturally, and physically strong America could bolster the West's ability to defeat political Islam and its radical left supporters.

In the short term, we should support the complete defeat of the oppressive theocracy in Iran, as initiated by the Trump administration's Maximum Pressure Campaign. We should stop its interference in Iraq, Syria, Yemen, Lebanon, and throughout Africa and Latin America. We must disable Iran's nuclear facilities and ballistic missile program. We should send aid to Iran's various minorities, who make up almost half of its population, and encourage them to set up autonomous zones. If we fail to implement needed strategies, the ayatollahs will win.

At least, we have achieved energy independence. That has been a long-sought and seemingly never-achievable goal for US national security and economic stability. The Trump administration has finally achieved it. There is more to do. Our energy independence can be extended to create a sphere of interactive international energy independence if we can intensify the development of energies such as solar, wave, geothermal, nuclear, hydrogen, natural gas, electromobility, ethanol, and biofuels. In the chicken-egg debate about planning for energy independence, the chicken comes first; that is, the fuel source must be strategically available before compatible alternative-fuel vehicles be can manufactured. The easiest way to make this happen is to convert public gas stations into fuel stations dispensing multiple fluids, gases, and electricity. There is no magic single replacement. It will probably take a symphony of alternative fuels before we see a difference. Since scrappage rates suggest that old cars enjoy an 11-year life before being sold off, starting tomorrow means a decade-long undertaking.

Cultural remedies are required to defeat cultural enemies. The US and other Western-style democracies should prevent the abuse of our unique laws that guarantee freedom of expression and the media. This freedom can be weaponized.

The Red and Green alliance of socialists and Islamists is not the only one to be counterchecked. Both White and Black supremacist parties and organizations, whether operating openly or in the shadows, need to be banned or made inert. Likewise, we need laws banning organizations that use riots or violence to intimidate the populace into submission. America saw such intimidation and violence in city after city during 2020. But our reaction must not be reactionary. We should employ successful tactics such as defining hate crimes, as is done in the US, Canada, and Europe, and banning the use of symbols and parties that project Nazism, as is done in Germany. But these tools must be used with care; otherwise, we do our enemies' work for them. Free expression is the oxygen of democracy. Before we restrict any of it, we must ensure we do not suffocate our freedoms.

The multifront war requires a multifront strategy to achieve victory. But a victory which tatters our liberties, our values, and our culture means we will have lost. We want to win—but we must win our multifront war correctly.

Afterword:
When the Smoke of 9/11 Cleared
Rachel Ehrenfeld

Al-Qaeda's attacks on the United States on September 11, 2001 marked a change in Kenneth Abramowitz's life. This book is the result of his nineteen year-long quest to examine, analyze, and understand the origins and growth of the evil ideology that instructs its followers to destroy Western civilization. He discovered that the Muslim Brotherhood, with its ideology of political Islam, or Islamism, were the instigators. These findings led him to further examine additional threats to the US and the West.

Political Islam or Islamism, like Nazism and Communism, rejects democracy, justice, free markets, and peace according to Western principles. Advocates of political Islam claim that Judeo-Christian and Western values are unjust and should, therefore, be replaced by the more just Islamic system. The promoters of political Islam have been using Western political jargon to convince the West that the Muslim Brotherhood's Islamism is just another moderate political—not religious—movement. Thus, their aggressive proselytizing and violent actions in the service of imposing their dictates have been met with little if any resistance for many decades.

The September 11, 2001 attacks forced us to consider that Islamism—not Muslims—might not be as peaceful as advertised. But we failed to seize the opportunity to find ways to contain the Islamist menace. Instead, our view of ourselves as unjust, promoted by the Left and the Islamists, had further weakened us. It is no accident that the War on Terror was the conceptual result of 9/11. President George W. Bush was either inept or unwilling to acknowledge the true enemy was the evil supremacist ideology of political Islam. The result of the failure to declare a war on Islamism led to further attacks by Islamist terrorists, and the advancement of political correctness, which introduced new restrictions on our freedom of speech. Ascertaining the obvious, that al-Qaeda and their ilk were Muslim terrorists, was suddenly met with wide criticism.

Oppressive Islamic countries, led by Saudi Arabia—the main sponsor of al-Qaeda—and the Muslim Brotherhood's affiliates in the West, asserted that Muslims cannot be terrorists because "Islam is the religion of peace." Since the US and other Western nations feared further attacks and unrest, and since the US and most of the world's economies were dependent on oil from Saudi Arabia and other Muslim countries, the Islamists got their way. The muzzling of our freedom of expression was reinforced with lawfare campaigns against real and imagined discrimination and profiling. The Muslim Brotherhood's affiliates in the US, foremost among them the Council on American-Islamic Relations, have been leading the charge. President Barack Hussein Obama validated the Islamists' claims in statements that reinforced the false narrative that political Islam is moderate. He supported Islamist leaders' claims that Islamic terrorism is an anomaly, often justified as a revolt against American and Western aggression and injustice, not only in Muslim countries but also against Muslims in the West.

European and US leadership's submissiveness to Islamic demands have been illustrated by their response to the violent Islamists' attacks on free speech after the publications of cartoons of the prophet Mohammad in Denmark. The Danes apologized. French president Jacques Chirac condemned all "overt provocations" that could inflame passions. "Anything that can hurt the convictions of someone else, in particular religious convictions, should be avoided," he said. And the supposed leader of the free world, US President Obama, declared in 2012 at the UN's General Assembly: "The future must not belong to those who slander the prophet of Islam."

Cartoons have long been used by different cultures to express political commentary. Not in Islam. So, after the Danish newspaper *Jyllands-Posten* published the cartoons of Muhammad on September 30, 2005, large well-funded and coordinated groups of Muslims rioted for many months around the world, especially in Europe.

Death threats forced the cartoonist and the publisher into hiding. Muslim-majority countries boycotted Danish products, and mobs attacked Danish and other Western diplomatic missions, raided churches, and killed more than 250 Christians.

The Islamists who have settled in Denmark and other European nations, whose numbers have increased greatly by waves of illegal migrants from the Middle East, Africa, and Asia, refuse to accept the Western traditions and laws of their host countries. Instead, guided by political Islamic organizations, they are creating alternative societies which they hope will eventually impose Sharia. These groups claimed the violent demonstrations erupted because the cartoons were an insult to Muhammed and Islam. Everywhere they clamored for and received apologies and even reparations.

The Islamists' suppression of free expression succeeded. Most European and even major US publications refrained from republishing the Mohammed cartoons, except for the satirical French magazine *Charlie Hebdo*, which on February 9, 2006 reprinted most of the *Jyllands-Posten*'s cartoons. Its cover featured Muhammad wearing a bomb-shaped turban with a lit fuse. The magazine's publishers received death threats, but did not relent and, in November 2011, published additional cartoons depicting Muhammad. The offices of the magazine were firebombed, and its website was attacked. And on January 7, 2015, members of the Arabian Peninsula branch of al-Qaeda attacked *Charlie Hebdo*'s offices in Paris, killing 12 employees of the magazine and injuring 11 others.

While Western political leaders strongly condemned the murderous attack on *Charlie Hebdo*, once again, they failed to condemn the political Islamic groups that continue to proselytize, indoctrinate, and incite their members to undermine Western values and institutions and impose Sharia everywhere.

This subversive religious movement, which masquerades as a secular political faction, established an arrangement of convenience with the fast-growing Marxist and Maoist Left that also seeks to undermine and destroy the US, which is still more free than other countries and the only remaining superpower in the world. Both groups target the US Constitution, American values and traditions, as well as its economic and social systems.

Following al-Qaeda's attack on 9/11, the US and other Western nations joined Israel's efforts to protect themselves from terrorist attacks. New, sophisticated technologies to better survey, identify, and monitor potential terrorist attacks were developed. However, the more sophisticated surveillance technologies became, the more infringements on privacy in the name of security were imposed. The general public reluctantly accepted these intrusions as the new reality.

Left-leaning media in the US and the West have crafted new constraints on free speech and expression, dictating what we can and cannot say. This prevents us from exposing them, as well as other enemies. Moreover, the unpatriotic, deceitful executives of America's foremost high-tech companies, such as

Google, Facebook, YouTube, and Twitter, who have developed technologies that not only censor what we say but also conceal and delete the information, are also limiting and doctoring data critical to our survival and wellbeing.

The effectiveness of manipulating the information available on the world's leading search engines, which are based in the US, did not escape the attention of our main adversaries: China, Russia, North Korea, and Iran. They succeeded in penetrating the systems and have been exploiting them to disseminate disinformation that assists both the Left's and the Islamists' efforts in undermining the US and the West.

Recent testimonies in the US Congress by Big Tech whistleblowers, as well as Allum Bokhari's book *Deleted*, have exposed how these companies, which enjoy the unique freedoms afforded in the US, have married algorithms with Artificial Intelligence (AI) to spy on every individual. They use their findings to choose the most effective tools to undermine our freedoms and our values. Claiming to be the facilitators of free speech and impartial distributors of information, they have become censors. They are even deleting evidentiary material of maleficence by the enemies of freedom and democracy.

For example, videos of horrific torture and murder committed by members of radical Islamic groups, such as al-Qaeda, Hamas, ISIS and Hezbollah, and incitement online to riot, loot, and murder by members of the Marxist-influenced Black Lives Matter movement and the anarchist Antifa movement, were initially listed by Google and available on YouTube, Twitter, and other online media outlets. However, since the election of Donald Trump as President of the US, and especially since the outbreak of the Wuhan coronavirus (COVID-19), most such evidence has been deleted. Twitter and the other outlets have been censoring and canceling statements and even accounts of those whose views differ from or oppose the prevailing progressive Left and Islamist views.

Mr. Abramowitz studied the US and the West's reaction to these and other geopolitical threats and found them wanting. This book is the result of his efforts to find strategies to protect the US and the West from the enemies of individual and economic freedom.

Dr. Rachel Ehrenfeld
New York City
October 2, 2020

Dr. Rachel Ehrenfeld is director, founder, and president of American Center for Democracy and its Economic Warfare Institute, and author of several books, including Funding Evil: How Terrorism is Financed, and How to Stop It.

Further Reading

Any student of the threat analysis explored in *The Multifront War* could consult many bookshelves to gain further insight. There are too many to mention here, but these titles offer insights into some of the many lines of thought—pro and con—that intersect the threats in the multifront war.

Attkisson, Sharyl. The Smear: *How Shady Political Operatives and Fake News Control What You See, What You Think, and How You Vote.*

Autry, Greg & Peter Navarro. *Death by China.*

Bailey, Norman A. et al. *The Grand Strategy That Won the Cold War.*

Bergen, Peter. *United States of Jihad: Who are America's Homegrown Terrorists, and How do We stop Them?.*

Black, Edwin. *Banking on Baghdad: Inside Iraq's 7,000-Year History of War, Profit, and Conflict.*

Black, Edwin. *Financing the Flames: How Tax-Exempt and Public Money Fuel a Culture of Confrontation and Terrorism in Israel.*

Bostom, Andrew G. *The Legacy of Jihad: Islamic Holy War and the Fate of Non-Muslims.*

Burr, Millard & Robert O. Collins. *Alms for Jihad.*

Calvert, John. *Sayyid Qutb and the Origins of Radical Islamism.*

Chang, Gordon G. *The Great U.S.-China Tech War.*

Coughlin, Stephen. *Catastrophic Failure: Blindfolding America in the Face of Jihad.*

Dunleavy, Patrick T. *The Fertile Soil of Jihad: Terrorism's Prison Connection.*

Ehrenfeld, Rachel. *Evil Money: The Inside Story of Money Laundering & Corruption in Government, Banks & Business.*

Ehrenfeld, Rachel. *Funding Evil: How Terrorism is Financed and How to Stop It.*

Emerson, Steven. *Jihad Incorporated: A Guide to Militant Islam in the US.*

Fleitz, Fred, Gordon G. Chang, et al. *Warning Order: China Prepares for Conflict, and Why We Must Do the Same.*

Freedman, Ilana. *Tablighi Jama'at: Gateway to Jihad.*

Furchtgott-Roth, Diana & Jared Meyer. *Disinherited: How Washington Is Betraying America's Young.*

Gertz, Bill. *Deceiving the Sky: Inside Communist China's Drive for Global Supremacy.*

Groiss, Arnon & Nethanel Toobian, ed & trans. *The War Curriculum in Iranian Schoolbooks.*

Haqqani, Husan. *Pakistan: Between Mosque and Military.*

Hohmann, Leo. *Stealth Invasion: Muslim Conquest Through Immigration & Resettlement.*

Humire, Joseph & Ilan Berman, eds. *Iran's Strategic Penetration of Latin America.*

Ibrahim, Raymond. *Sword and Scimitar: Fourteen Centuries of War Between Islam and the West.*

Kagan, Frederick W. *Finding the Target: The Transformation of American Military Policy.*

Karsh, Efraim. *Islamic Imperialism: A History.*

Kirby, Stephen M. *Islamic Doctrine Versus the U.S. Constitution: The Dilemma for Muslim Public Officials.*

LeBlanc, Jim. *Real Risk Management for the Electrical Grid.*

Lewis, Bernard. *The Crisis of Islam: Holy War and Unholy Terror.*

Lewis, Bernard. *What Went Wrong? The Clash between Islam and Modernity in the Middle East.*

Liang, Qiao and Wang Xiangsui. *Unrestricted Warfare.*

Lokam, Shivaji. *The Fall of Western Civilization: How Liberalism is Destroying the West from Within.*

Lukianoff, Greg. *Unlearning Liberty: Campus Censorship and The End of American Debate.*

MacDonald, Heather. *The Diversity Delusion: How Race and Gender Pandering Corrupt the University and Undermine Our Culture.*

Marcus, Itamar & Nan Jacques Zilberdik. *Deception: Betraying the Peace Process.*

Mawyer, Martin. *Twilight in America: The Untold Story of Islamic Terrorist Training Camps Inside America.*

McCarthy, Andrew C. *The Grand Jihad: How Islam and the Left Sabotage America.*

Mitchell, Richard Paul. *The Society of the Muslim Brothers.*

Mohammed, Yasmine. *Unveiled: How Western Liberals Empower Radical Islam.*

Mosher, Steven W. *Bully of Asia: Why China's Dream is the New Threat to World Order.*

Murray, Douglas. *The Strange Death of Europe: Immigration, Identity, Islam.*

Neumann, Jonathan. *To Heal the World? How the Jewish Left Corrupts Judaism and Endangers Israel.*

Owen IV, John M. *Confronting Political Islam: Six Lessons from the West's Past.*

Peters, Ralph. *Endless War: Middle-Eastern Islam Vs. Western Civilization.*

Phares, Walid. *Future Jihad: Terrorist Strategies against America.*

Phares, Walid. *The Choice: Trump vs. Obama-Biden in U.S. Foreign Policy.*

Phares, Walid. *The Confrontation: Winning the War against Future Jihad.*

Phares, Walid. *The Lost Spring: U.S. Policy in the Middle East and Catastrophes to Avoid.*

Phares, Walid. *The War of Ideas: Jihadism against Democracy.*

Phillips, Melanie. *Londonistan: How Britain Is Creating a Terror State Within.*

Pillsbury, Michael. *China's Secret Strategy to Replace America as the Global Superpower.*

Podhoretz, Norman. *World War IV: The Long Struggle Against Islamofascism.*

Pry, Peter. *The EMP Manhattan Project.*

Qutb, Sayyid. *Milestones.*

Rahman, Saif. *The Islamist Delusion: From Islamist to Cultural Muslim Humanist.*

Rectenwald, Michael. *Google Archipelago: The Digital Gulag and the Simulation of Freedom.*

Rhode, Harold. *Modern Islamic Warfare.*

Sekulow, Jay. *Unholy Alliance: The Agenda Iran, Russia, and Jihadists Share for Conquering the World.*

Siddiqi, Shamin A. *Methodology of Dawah.*

Stakelbeck, Erick. *The Brotherhood: America's Next Great Enemy.*

Ward, Jonathan D.T. *China's Vision of Victory.*

Warraq, Ibn. *The Islam in Islamic Terrorism: The Importance of Beliefs, Ideas, and Ideology.*

Warraq, Ibn. *What the Koran Really Says: Language, Text, and Commentary.*

Wood, David. *The Two Faces of Islam: Saudi Fundamentalism and Its Role in Terrorism.*

Ye'or, Bat. *Europe, Globalization, and The Coming Universal Caliphate.*

About the Author

Threat analyst KENNETH ABRAMOWITZ is managing General Partner and co-founder of NGN Capital, a half-billion-dollar worldwide healthcare venture capital fund. He joined NGN from the Carlyle Group in New York where he was managing director from 2001 to 2003, focused on US buyout opportunities in the healthcare industry. Before joining Carlyle, he was a healthcare industry analyst for Sanford C. Bernstein & Co., Inc. from 1997 to 2000. For his industry work, he was installed in the Wall Street Analyst Hall of Fame with a rank of 15 out of 15,000 analysts. He lectures worldwide on the issues of democracy.

Made in the USA
Middletown, DE
15 October 2020